TOUCHING
THE JAGUAR

OTHER BOOKS BY JOHN PERKINS

The New Confessions of an Economic Hit Man

The Secret History of the American Empire

Hoodwinked

Confessions of an Economic Hit Man

Shapeshifting

The World Is As You Dream It

Spirit of the Shuar

Psychonavigation

The Stress-Free Habit

TOUCHING
THE JAGUAR

TRANSFORMING FEAR INTO ACTION
TO CHANGE YOUR LIFE AND THE WORLD

JOHN PERKINS

Berrett–Koehler Publishers, Inc.

Berrett-Koehler Publishers, Inc.
1333 Broadway, Suite 1000
Oakland, CA 94612-1921
Tel: (510) 817-2277
Fax: (510) 817-2278
www.bkconnection.com

ORDERING INFORMATION

Quantity sales. Special discounts are available on quantity purchases by corporations, associations, and others. For details, contact the "Special Sales Department" at the Berrett-Koehler address above.

Individual sales. Berrett-Koehler publications are available through most bookstores. They can also be ordered directly from Berrett-Koehler: Tel: (800) 929-2929; Fax: (802) 864-7626; www.bkconnection.com.

Orders for college textbook / course adoption use. Please contact Berrett-Koehler: Tel: (800) 929-2929; Fax: (802) 864-7626.

Distributed to the U.S. trade and internationally by Penguin Random House Publisher Services.

Berrett-Koehler and the BK logo are registered trademarks of Berrett-Koehler Publishers, Inc.

Printed in the United States of America

Berrett-Koehler books are printed on long-lasting acid-free paper. When it is available, we choose paper that has been manufactured by environmentally responsible processes. These may include using trees grown in sustainable forests, incorporating recycled paper, minimizing chlorine in bleaching, or recycling the energy produced at the paper mill.

Library of Congress Cataloging-in-Publication Data
Names: Perkins, John, 1945- author.
Title: Touching the jaguar : transforming fear into action to change your life and the world / John Perkins.
Description: First edition. | Oakland, CA : Berrett-Koehler Publishers, [2020] | Includes bibliographical references and index.
Identifiers: LCCN 2020002026 | ISBN 9781523089864 (hardcover) | ISBN 9781523089871 (pdf) | ISBN 9781523089888 (epub)
Subjects: LCSH: Perkins, John, 1945- | United States. National Security Agency—Biography. | Economists—United States—Biography. | Energy consultants—United States—Biography. | Intelligence officers—United States—Biography. | Corporations, American—Corrupt practices. | Shamanism—Amazon River Region. | Social action. | Social change. | Environmental responsibility.
Classification: LCC UB271.U52 P472 2020 | DDC 332/.042092 [B]—dc23
LC record available at https://lccn.loc.gov/2020002026

First Edition
27 26 25 24 23 22 21 20   10 9 8 7 6 5 4 3 2 1

Book producer and text designer: Happenstance Type-O-Rama
Cover designer: Wes Youssi, M80 Design

To the Indigenous people who are blazing
the trail to a future our children will want to
inherit, to Kiman Lucas, who has held my hand
as I walk that trail, and to my grandson, Grant
Miller, who inspires me to keep walking.

CONTENTS

PART 1 • The Perception Trap *1968–1970*

I had no idea that he was suggesting that I might be upgraded from spy to economic hit man.

PART 2 • The Death Economy *1970–1987*

It was a system that was bound to fail, to kill itself—what economists would later define as a Death Economy.

PART 3 • Changing the Dream *1987–1993*

The world is as you dream it. Your people dreamed of huge factories, tall buildings, as many cars as there are raindrops in this river. Now you begin to see that your dream is a nightmare.

PART 4 • Uniting the Eagle and the Condor *1993*

The prophecy says that five hundred years later—now—the opportunity arises for the Eagle and the Condor to fly together, to mate, and to produce a new offspring, higher consciousness.

PART 5 • Confronting the Jaguar *1993*

They said they had dreamed on this, that their shamans had gone deep into the meaning of their visions, and they had concluded that they have to touch us—their people have to touch our people—initiate contact with the very thing they most fear.

PART 6 • The Legend of the Evias *1994–1995*

You must ask yourself about the Evias in your life. What scares you? . . . What must you do to change this? . . . You must do this alone. No one can help you. Only by doing that will you avoid going to war with yourself.

PART 7 • Creating a Life Economy *1993–2017*

This Life Economy cleans up pollution, regenerates devastated environments, recycles, and develops new technologies that benefit people and nature. Businesses that pay returns to investors who invest in an economy that is itself a renewable resource become the success stories.

PART 8 • Decolonization *2017–Present*

We are the Elder Siblings . . . Our job is to show you, the Younger Siblings, about taking care of our sacred mother, the earth.

In these tracks, feel the jaguar that blocks your people. And feel the jaguar that is your ally for change.

Introduction

Meeting the Jaguar

"Touching the jaguar" means that you can identify your fears and barriers, confront them, alter your perceptions about them, accept their energy, and take actions to change yourself and the world.

I STARTED TO WRITE THIS BOOK as a bridge that would connect my previous books on Indigenous cultures, including *Shapeshifting*, to those on global economics, including *Confessions of an Economic Hit Man*. I had no idea that it would turn out to be that and also become much more.

My journey began in 1968 when, as a US Peace Corps volunteer, I was sent into the Amazon jungles of Ecuador to form credit and savings cooperatives—something I soon learned was impossible. Once there, I met Indigenous people who were coming into contact with my world, the industrialized world, for the first time. They lived in harmony with nature and yet were constantly fighting their neighbors to protect their territories. Animosities dated back centuries. Then something unexpected happened.

Foreign oil and mining companies arrived and began to destroy their forests.

The Indigenous people realized that their only hope was to "touch the jaguar."

For the Aztec, Inca, and Maya, the jaguar represented power and valor, the epitome of physical strength and mental awareness. Today, in the Amazon, touching a jaguar during a vision quest symbolizes the courage to overcome doubts, challenge enemies, and break through obstacles. Because it can see through the blackness of night and has excellent peripheral vision, the jaguar is said to embody our ability to look into the dark parts of our souls, view all that is around us, determine our path to the future, and take actions that will guide us along that path. Local stories tell of lost hunters led back to the trail by a jaguar and of jaguars that saved lives by giving animals they had killed to incapacitated people starving in the jungle. Although the jaguar is dangerous, it is also known as a gift giver; its gifts may be physical, psychological, or spiritual.

An Amazonian shaman once told me, "'Touching the jaguar' means that you can identify your fears and barriers, confront them, alter your perceptions about them, accept their energy, and take actions to change yourself and the world."

When the big oil and mining companies arrived, the people of the Amazon realized that the thing they most feared was no longer their neighbors; it was the invasion of their lands by foreign corporations. They had to confront that fear. They had to touch the jaguar that would give them the gift of wisdom and strength needed to break through the barriers of old biases and traditions. They had to change their perceptions about their neighbors; they had to take actions to form alliances with age-old enemies to protect their world.

Then they understood that the real threat was bigger than those companies; it came from the mind-sets of the nations that ravage the earth for its resources. They saw that their lands were in danger of being commandeered by outsiders who wanted to take control of their economies, lifestyles, minds, environment, and even their forms of government—in other words, outsiders who were determined to colonize them.

The newly formed alliances took it upon themselves to go to the thing they most feared—us, people from the world of the colonizers. They asked me to deliver a message to those people about the urgency of shifting the destructive patterns of the industrialized civilizations. They requested that I bring them a small group of individuals who had the capacity to create networks for delivering this message globally.

Once our group arrived in the Amazon, we were challenged by Indigenous people to transform our perceptions of how we relate to them and to our home, the earth. They asked us to replace old values and systems based on social hierarchies and exploitation with ones that honor egalitarianism and compassion; they urged us to decolonize our own minds, economies, and lifestyles. And they counseled us to stop defining ourselves in terms of "us versus them." They pointed out that if they, who had been enemies for so long, could join forces to protect their territory, then so could people from different countries, cultures, and economic and political systems, like the Americans, Russians, and Chinese. Old antagonisms could be dropped to confront a graver danger. They challenged us to join forces to create a world our children and grandchildren will want to inherit.

It became obvious that what the Indigenous people were asking us to do was something they themselves had already done. They had altered their perceptions to change their reality; now they were urging us to do the same.

While writing this book, I discovered that I was telling stories of true events that are so bizarre they seem like fiction. Amazonian people who were officially uncontacted when I first entered their territory came to see something about us that we did not understand about ourselves. They recognized that our drive to colonize others was causing us serious harm. It was creating a global economic system that was consuming itself into extinction, a Death Economy. Driven by a goal of maximizing short-term profits, regardless of the social and environmental costs, this Death Economy had been aggressively promoted by economists and politicians in the 1970s and 1980s. Prior to that, when I was in business school in the late 1960s, CEOs had been taught to take good care of their employees, suppliers, and customers and the communities where their businesses operated and to earn reasonable returns for their investors.

As a former economic hit man who contributed to the expansion of the Death Economy and as one who has lived with the people of the Amazon and apprenticed with shamans, I've come to understand my obligation to change my own perceptions and to do everything I can to help transform dysfunctional systems into ones that will serve us—all life on this planet. I take heart in the knowledge that for most of human history our ancestors created social-governmental-economic systems that focused on long-term benefits for people and nature and were themselves renewable resources. The Indigenous people who still live that way were and are urging us to transform the Death Economy into one that cleans up pollution, regenerates destroyed ecosystems, recycles, and creates technologies that restore resources and that benefit, rather than ravage, the environment—a Life Economy.

I want to make it clear that I don't idealize or villainize individual Indigenous people. My own experiences have taught me that there are treacherous and virtuous ones, brutal and peaceful ones, and psychotic and well-balanced ones, just as there are in all cultures. What I respect is their communal commitments to the long term. Their philosophies and actions are dedicated to taking care of their environments, their cultures, and their offspring. The stories that Indigenous people have long told their children—and now us—such as the Prophecy of the Eagle and the Condor, the Mayan Prophecy of 2012, and the Legend of Etsaa and the Evias, offer powerful teachings about the ability each of us has to overcome obstacles, to change our perceptions, and in so doing, to alter reality. In this regard, those stories have much in common with the myths embedded in cultures around the world and with the practices of modern psychotherapy and quantum physics.

This book discusses the damage I perpetrated as an economic hit man and the reality-changing lessons I learned in the Amazon. It goes on to describe the work I've done for the past forty years to meet my jaguars and apply the lessons I learned to alleviate the harm I helped cause. It delves into the problems that current greed and short-term perspectives are causing. And, perhaps most important of all, it presents actions that you, the reader, can take to change your life and help all of us humans live more harmoniously with nature and each other.

Prologue

American Colonialism, Guatemala, 1993

Empires had been colonizing tribes and nations for centuries, appropriating their economies, their lands, their peoples, their governments, and their minds . . . in the name of religion, civilization, and westernization. This time it had been done under the subterfuge of spreading democracy. . . .

"EIGHT MEN WERE ASSASSINATED here last week." The Land Rover slowed into the curve. "Guatemalan soldiers stopped a bus at this very spot." Jorge, our Mayan-to-Spanish interpreter, peered over the back of his seat at Lynne Twist, who was behind him, and then at me, next to her. "They dragged those eight Mayan men off. Shot and killed them. One by one." He pointed at a cluster of scrawny bushes just outside his window. "Right there. Last week."

I stared out at the bushes. My heart raced. The Land Rover drove on.

"The civil war still rages," Jorge continued. "It's lasted more than thirty years." He glanced from Lynne to me. "Those soldiers were trained by the US military," he stared at me, "to help the rich families here who want to destroy the Mayan culture and support exploitation of our resources by US companies. It's the latest example of American colonialism."

American colonialism. My intestines knotted.

"Genocide," Lynne said. She too was watching me.

I glanced through the window on my side of the Land Rover, fighting back the sickening taste of bile. I'd been an economic hit man, an ally of those rich families Jorge talked about, a person whose job it was to promote colonialism. As I would later write in *Confessions of an Economic Hit Man*,

> *Economic hit men (EHMs) are highly paid professionals who cheat countries around the globe out of trillions of dollars. They funnel money from the World Bank, the US Agency for International Development (USAID), and other foreign-aid organizations into the coffers of huge corporations and the pockets of a few wealthy families who control the planet's natural resources. Their tools include fraudulent financial reports, rigged elections, payoffs, extortion, sex, and murder. They play a game as old as empire, but one that has taken on new and terrifying dimensions during this time of globalization.*

> *I should know; I was an EHM.*[1]

I had officially retired from the EHM ranks in 1980, but here I was, thirteen years later, back in Guatemala. I was working as a consultant to a corporation that was an integral part of the system Jorge had identified as colonialism. At the same time, during this trip I was serving on the board of a nonprofit organization that helped the Mayan people during this terrible civil war. The irony struck me. I justified my consulting work as a way to support my family. I told myself that I would convince my corporate clients to be environmentally and socially conscious of what they were doing in Guatemala and elsewhere. However, the facts about the Maya challenged my attempts at justifying my position.

An estimated two hundred thousand Maya had been killed or "disappeared" by a government that was backed by Washington and US corporations. Many more had fled as refugees.[2] Dozens of villages had been razed. Families had been driven off their small farms and replaced by large American-owned or -supported agribusinesses. In addition to Maya, victims also included student activists, labor leaders, and Catholic priests who participated in nonviolent movements. More people were killed in this conflict than in any other twentieth century Latin American war—a fact that was unknown by most Americans.[3]

Now I was taking Lynne into the mountains that were the stronghold of the very people we EHMs had exploited and killed. "Yes, genocide," I repeated. I tried to swallow away that sour taste in my mouth, tried to fight down the feelings of guilt I felt over the things I'd done and the fear of what lay ahead of us. I stared through the window at the bleak mountains and the road as we sped away from those bushes where the unforgivable had happened.

"Sometimes it's hard to be an American," Lynne said. She had been introduced to me as a philanthropic activist and chief fundraiser for the Hunger Project. This was before she'd written her bestselling book, *The Soul of Money*, received the United Nations Woman of Distinction award, become an advisor to the Nobel Women's Institute, been featured on *Oprah*, and been honored with many other accolades.

It was also before colonialism took on the appalling and tragic aspects that would emerge in the second decade of the twenty-first century. The world would be haunted by extreme anti-immigrant attitudes and actions, the growth of white supremist and nationalist movements, increasing income inequality, escalating social and community divisions, and the denial of climate change. It also was a time before the growing power and influence of China around the world.

Lynne touched my arm. "What does it feel like for you—being back here?"

I didn't know what to say. I didn't want to admit to the sour taste in my mouth, the ache in my heart, or the knot in my stomach. I felt torn between my job as a corporate hit man and my role as a defender of Indigenous rights. "Weird," I said at last. "Very weird." Then I looked at her. "Like a man caught between two worlds."

I studied the road ahead and the dark clouds beyond that had gathered over the mountains, our destination. I thought about the role I'd played in colonizing the world on behalf of the United States and its corporations. Empires had been colonizing tribes and nations for centuries, appropriating their economies, their lands, their peoples, their governments, and their minds. It had been done in the name of religion, civilization, and westernization. This time it had been done under the subterfuge of spreading democracy, even when "spreading democracy" meant overthrowing or assassinating democratically elected presidents in places as diverse as Iran and Panama—if those presidents and their policies appeared to threaten US businesses or hegemony—while at the same time defending brutal dictators in places as diverse as Chile and Saudi Arabia who did support the US. And it had produced what we would come to realize was a failed economic system.

Lynne's hand on my arm brought me back to the present. "You worked for the Guatemalan government during the war here, didn't you?" Lurking beneath those words, I heard an accusation: *The one that kills Maya.*

"Well . . ." I searched for something to say. "I never actually worked for the government. Not really anyway." I looked at her and then back through the window, as I tried to figure out how to describe my complicated story.

I'd grown up the son of a teacher at a New Hampshire boarding school for wealthy boys. I'd done what was expected of me, received a full scholarship to college, and scaled the corporate ladder to become chief economist at Chas. T. Main (MAIN), a Boston-based consulting firm, before I turned thirty. Disillusioned and distraught by the consequences of the work I did there, I quit after only a decade at that job. I then became a writer and teacher and now was a board member of Katalysis, a nonprofit that helped Mayan women organize themselves into microcredit cooperatives. I knew that she had read that much in my bio. But how much more had she learned? Even after leaving the chief economist role behind, I'd been silent all these years about the fact that, in my case, "chief economist" was a cover for "economic hit man." I'd tried to keep that fact hidden.

"I was a consultant," I told Lynne, avoiding her eyes. "In the '70s I came here to arrange World Bank loans." I turned toward her and forced a smile. "That's about it."

"I thought you were here recently . . ."

"Oh yes. Of course . . ." Where had she heard that? "But just as an advisor to a US engineering company, Stone and Webster." I paused.

She sat there beside me, waiting . . .

"I was supposed to negotiate a deal with a Guatemalan company, to develop a geothermal project," I added.

"Guatemalan company?" Her voice seemed to ask the unspoken question.

"Yes, that company was owned by one of the ruling families." I nodded toward the back of Jorge's head. "Not something I can talk about right now."

She smiled gently. "I understand, but if you do feel like talking, I'd love to hear your story . . ." She sat back, closed her eyes, and then said, "Sometimes it helps to talk."

Hearing those words, I realized that I did want to talk. For the first time, in the back of a Land Rover, speeding toward the mountains, I began to tell my story . . .

PART 1

The Perception Trap

1968–1970

*I had no idea that he was suggesting
that I might be upgraded from
spy to economic hit man.*

1

WELCOME TO THE MIRACLE

DURING THE SUMMER OF 1968, before my last year at Boston University's business school, I married my best friend, Ann. I was adamantly opposed to the Vietnam War, although I did not consider myself a pacifist. My dad and uncles had fought in World War II and I liked to believe that I would have done the same. Mine was a philosophical objection. It reflected Muhammad Ali's pronouncement: "I ain't got no quarrel with them Vietcong."[1]

Ann's father was high up in the Department of the Navy and his best friend was a top executive at the National Security Agency, the country's least known—and by most accounts, largest—spy organization. Realizing that a job at the NSA could earn me a draft deferment, I asked "Uncle Frank" (as Ann referred to him) for help. He arranged for an NSA recruiter to fast-track me.

I endured a series of grueling interviews and psychological tests while I was strapped to a lie detector. When I admitted that I opposed the war, the interviewers surprised me by not pursuing this subject. Instead, they focused on my upbringing as the son of a teacher at an all-boys boarding school, my attitudes toward my puritanical parents, the emotions I felt growing up cash poor on a campus populated by so many wealthy, often hedonistic, preppies. Many of their questions zeroed in on my feelings about the absence of women during my adolescent years and the awkwardness I felt around them, my shyness, and my determination to get even with those wealthy preppies who came back after Christmas vacation bragging about the orgies they'd attended while I'd spent my days shooting baskets by myself in the school gymnasium. I would later come to understand that my obsession with women, my desire for material success, and my anger marked me as a man who could be hooked. The NSA didn't care about my attitudes toward a war they knew the US was losing. All that mattered to them was that I was vulnerable; I could be seduced.

Not long after those interviews, Uncle Frank called to tell me that I was "in."

The day after I received the NSA's offer, I happened to stumble into a seminar given at BU by a Peace Corps recruiter. He enthusiastically described Peace Corps projects that helped build bridges between people in other countries and Americans and ones that brought potable water and other benefits to communities that lacked the resources to develop them themselves. He also mentioned that Peace Corps volunteers were eligible for draft deferments—like NSA employees. He described several places in the world that especially needed volunteers. One of these was the Amazon rain forest where, he pointed out, Indigenous people lived very much as they had in pre-Columbus North America.

Growing up in a family that reached back to the 1600s in New England, I'd been fascinated by stories of frontier life, the French and Indian and Revolutionary Wars, and especially the information I devoured about the Abenaki people who had survived in the deep forests as hunters and gatherers—and attacked the settlements where my ancestors lived. I thrived on books like *The Last of the Mohicans*, *Northwest Passage*, *Drums Along the Mohawk*, and others about frontier warfare. Like many boys my age, I idolized Walt Disney's Davy Crockett. I dreamed of living that type of life. It never occurred to me as a child that these stories glorified colonization, a system, I've since learned, that occurs when a dominant group from a foreign culture takes control of local peoples to exploit their resources; steal their lands; manipulate their economies; enslave or abuse their men, women, and children; force religious beliefs, languages, and culture on them; and break their bodies through violence, imprisonment, and sometimes genocide. I was blinded by the tales fed to me by schools, books, and movies. As a project for my seventh-grade history class, I wrote a short novel about the war between the European settlers in my native New Hampshire and the Abenaki. True to my education, I portrayed the colonists as the heroes; yet my fascination with Abenaki culture was evident throughout my writings. My teacher took me aside to tell me that people still lived that way in the Amazon rain forests. She showed me a photo taken from a small plane of a man in feathered headdress and loin cloth standing next to a thatched roof hut in a forest clearing aiming his bow and arrow at the photographer in the low-flying plane. "I've got to go there," I told her back then. Sitting in the room listening to the Peace Corps recruiter, I remembered that moment and I thought, Now might be the time.

I called Uncle Frank.

"The Peace Corps? The Amazon." He chuckled. "Perfect. We can make sure you get there. You'll learn another language, receive training in intercultural and survival skills. After you finish, you can come work for us." He paused, then added, "Or you may end up employed by a private company instead of the government."

I had no idea that he was suggesting that I might be upgraded from spy to economic hit man—a term and concept I had never heard of and would not for a few more years. Back then, I could not have guessed that hundreds of men and women "consultants" who were paid by private companies served the interests of the US government and the rapidly expanding corporate empire.

Ann convinced me that she too wanted to visit the Amazon and liked the idea of serving her country and people who needed help. We joined the Peace Corps and were sent to eight weeks of courses in Spanish, credit and savings cooperatives, and hygiene at a training camp that had once been a nudist colony near Escondido, California. At the end, we were able to pass the rudimentary Spanish test. Without realizing it and although I have no reason to believe it was the Peace Corps' intent, I'd later come to see that I'd been prepped to carry the torch of colonialism later in my life.

They assigned us to a remote area in the Amazon rain forest of eastern Ecuador, known to most Ecuadorians as the "Oriente." Ann would teach basic childcare. Because of my business school education, I would develop credit and savings cooperatives. Some of the literature I found in the Boston Public Library referred to the region where we were headed as "Shuar Territory" and compared it to the early American frontier. Young Shuar men (one source claimed) could not be initiated into manhood or take a wife until they had killed and shrunken the head of an enemy. Pitched battles raged between various Shuar clans and against their common enemies, the neighboring Achuar.

As our plane flew toward Ecuador's capital, Quito, I grew increasingly excited. An Ecuadorian newspaper handed to me by a flight attendant featured a picture of a shrunken head with a caption that I translated as "Ecuador's Savages Attack Texaco Teams." Ferocious "Indians" pitted against the forces of civilization. This was right out of the books I'd read and the movies I'd seen. I was about to experience Davy Crockett's life. I would not realize how blatantly racist and imperialistic this view was until later when I would come to see that the Indigenous people were fighting to conserve their environment from the wanton destruction of oil exploitation. They were struggling to protect their lives and those of their children from government soldiers and petroleum company mercenaries.

Ann and I spent another week of cross-cultural training in Quito and then were sent to the Peace Corps regional office in Cuenca—a provincial Andean city that was abuzz with rumors about skirmishes between Texaco and the Indigenous people. After a few days there, our regional director, Jim, drove Ann and me to an open-air market.

"You'll catch the bus here. It'll be marked 'Fin del Camino,'" Jim said. "End of the Road." Then he gave us last minute instructions, adding, "It's not the official name of the community, but you'll know you're there when you see a sign welcoming you to 'El Milagro.'"

"The Miracle?" Ann asked. She looked skeptical.

"That's the translation." He laughed. "Don't take it too literally. It's quite a story, though. A lost and starving gold prospector wandered for days in the jungle before he was led to this community by, he said, the voice of an angel. He called the place a miracle and people have joked about it ever since."

Jim drove off, leaving us surrounded by a crowd of people who were dressed in ponchos, woolen skirts, and trousers and speaking Quichua,* the most common Indigenous language of the Andes. Many of them had pigs or goats tied to ropes they held or chickens penned inside crude wooden cages. Babies cried, staticky music blared from a speaker somewhere, roosters crowed, and dogs barked. The air was permeated by a pungent odor that suggested a combination of rotting fruits, feces, and fried pork.

Although we'd been in Cuenca for several days, we'd stuck to the charming colonial parts of town. This was our first experience in what was known in those days as "El Mercado Indio." I stared at Ann, dumbfounded, depressed. "This is unbelievable," I said, having no idea that there would come a time when I would appreciate this type of market as being true capitalism, as opposed to the predatory type that was sweeping the part of the world we referred to as developed and was creating a failing system that would be defined as a Death Economy.

"Yes." She gave a sigh. "I think we're lucky to be getting out of here, heading to the jungle."

Suddenly the other sounds were smothered by the loud and persistent honking of a horn. The crowd parted and the cab of a very old Ford truck appeared. Behind it, apparently fastened to what had once been the truck's frame, was a long, wooden box about as high as a man. Although painted like a rainbow interwoven with flowers, the colors were faded and plastered with mud. An irregular row of ragged holes had been cut into the side; they were covered by clear plastic to serve as windows. When it pulled to a stop, we saw the sign: "Fin del Camino."

"That's our bus?" Ann gasped.

Men, women, and children pushed past us, their pigs, goats, and chickens in tow, and climbed up into the wooden box.

---

* There are different ways of spelling and defining certain words and aspects of Indigenous cultures. I've used what seem to be the most common versions. In this book, "Quechua" denotes the majority of Indigenous people living in the Andes. "Quichua" is the language most of them speak in Ecuador (a somewhat different dialect from the "Quechua" of Peru). The Kichwa are an Amazonian culture who are related to those in the Andes and, unlike the Achuar and Shuar, speak a Quichua dialect. I avoid the term "tribe," replacing it with the more appropriate "culture" or in many cases the legally correct "nation," except when referring to the history of empires.

"Fin del Camino? Fin del Camino?" a man in a torn jacket yelled at me. I nodded.

He shoved people aside and hustled us up through the doorway of the bus and inside. We were greeted by the odor of urine and sweat. I peered down the rows of crude wooden benches crammed with passengers and their animals. I felt as if I'd been hit in the gut with a sledgehammer.

The man in the torn jacket spoke harshly in Quichua to an elderly couple sitting on the front bench. Without saying a word, they rose slowly and moved to the back of the bus. "Para los gringos," the man said and pointed at the vacated seat.

"Should we 'gringos' accept this?" Ann asked. "It seems wrong."

"It does feel elitist," I said. "But I think we ought to take it. They expect us to." I felt guilty admitting to our privileged status, but I wanted that front seat and quickly added, "The man who put us here might be insulted if we move. And he's probably the driver."

We sat down and spent the next several hours in that wooden box, along with the pigs, goats, and chickens—and people whose body odor was so strong that I imagined that some of them carried decaying corpses in the grimy burlap bags that lay on their laps or were heaped along the narrow aisle and on top of the overhead shelves.

We heard the word "gringos" frequently repeated, although we could not understand what they were saying about us because it was either spoken in Quichua or a Spanish that was so rapid as to be beyond our comprehension. However, the tone of their voices and the laughter suggested that we were the subjects of a good deal of joking.

Late in the afternoon, as the bus careened and skidded its way along the serpentine road, I grabbed our paper lunch bag, frantically handed Ann its contents, and vomited into it.

The woman behind me patted my back gently and, speaking softly in Quichua, handed Ann a small basket. The man beside her motioned with his hands that I could vomit into it. It was a gesture that spoke to the generosity that I would come to learn was a hallmark of Andean people. No matter how poor they were or how much they could have resented our privileges, they were compassionate and extremely giving.

"You know," Ann observed later, "this is the sort of travel millions of people around the world experience all the time. We in the US are very privileged. We take our amazing advantages for granted."

That bus ride, being given the front seat, my vomiting, and the kindness of the couple behind us humbled me. We were indeed privileged. I would remember it for the rest of my life.

The land of the high Andes was not what I'd expected. Rather than picturesque, it appeared desolate. The people who lived and farmed here faced what seemed like impossible odds. Sometimes we'd pass a tiny adobe hut and I'd catch a glimpse of workers in the nearby fields, bent over, laboring to grow corn along nearly perpendicular slopes. These scenes aroused in me more feelings of anxiety. Could I cope for the next two years with this country? Did I have the stamina these people had? The ability to endure? To survive? I was afraid that I could not handle the changes in lifestyle and attitudes that would be required of me.

I closed my eyes. I tried to put this place and what seemed like a dark future out of my mind. I forced myself to think about the Ecuadorian history I'd read in books before leaving the States. The people I'd seen outside through the plastic-covered holes in the bus, the Andean natives, had been conquered by the Inca who forced their language, economic system, and culture on them. After that, the Conquistadors defeated the Inca and brought in Catholicism, Spanish, and their form of feudalism. Then I had another thought—that the United States was trying to colonize Vietnam. While it was disturbing to consider that my country was following in the footsteps of violent empires, it also made me realize once again how fortunate I was not to be in Vietnam.

Our one night on the road was spent in a roadside "inn." Our room in the decrepit wooden building was reached by a rickety outside staircase and furnished with only a wobbly wooden stool and a wooden frame crisscrossed with rope netting. Thrown onto the ropes was a dirty, thin mattress that appeared to have been decorated by a mad artist obsessed with yellow stains. We unrolled our sleeping bags, spread them on the mattress, and fell into an exhausted sleep.

Late that night, I couldn't avoid the need to visit what I'd already seen was a foul and rat-infested outhouse. When my feet touched the floor, it moved. Cockroaches! I jerked my feet back onto the bed. Then, Ann's words about being privileged and taking our advantages for granted came to me. I tried to convince myself that they were harmless bugs and that everyone else undoubtedly was dealing with them. I lowered my feet and took a step, then another. My feet crunched their way through the cockroaches and down the stairs to the outhouse.

The next morning was shrouded in a mist that clung to the buildings and around the bus. Many of our fellow travelers greeted us with "Buenos días," pleasant smiles, and curious looks. I realized that, as foreign as they and all these experiences were for Ann and me, we were equally as foreign to them. At six feet, with curly light-brown hair, I towered above most of them. Ann's long reddish-blond hair, her jeans, and her high leather boots were like nothing any of them had ever witnessed before—except for the bus driver who assured us that he'd seen her in a Hollywood movie.

That day, our second, the bus made frequent stops to let people and animals off at paths that disappeared into the mist or at the occasional adobe hut. As the bus descended down the Andes toward the jungle, sometimes slipping precariously close to the edge of the dirt road that hung high above a violently cascading river, the homes grew scarcer. The scenery went from arid mountains to steep canyon walls covered in lush cloud forests. The homes changed to hand-hewn boards that were perpendicular, rather than parallel, to the ground.

After nearly two days of many stops and the night of cockroaches, the bus was empty, except for three drunken *mestizo* (people of Spanish and Indigenous heritage) men, Ann, and me. Around midday, it coughed to a standstill at a cluster of wooden hovels surrounded by dense forest.

Peering out, I saw that the road simply came to an end. It stopped at a wall of trees. The jungle took over. Judging from the piles of pickaxes and shovels and the one ancient bulldozer, this was a road construction camp. A group of ragged bearded men sat at a long board table, eating lunch. Their tattered clothes were caked with mud. Tethered to a crude hitching rail were a few horses next to a sign that read, "Para alquilar" (For rent).

We sat there at the front of the bus, not sure what to do. Our three drunk companions staggered past us with their burlap bags. Each of them shook our hands and muttered words I didn't understand but accepted as encouragement. They addressed me, as I would be addressed throughout my Peace Corps time in Ecuador, simply as "Mister Gringito" and Ann as "Mistera Gringita."

We climbed down from the bus. I went up to the table. The men were gawking at Ann as though they had never seen anything quite like her before. "Dónde está El Milagro?" I asked. (Where is El Milagro?) One of the men pointed at the horses. We headed for them.

"They're tiny," Ann said. "Not what I'd expected."

"Used to Ecuadorians, not us overgrown 'gringos.'" I turned to the man who seemed to be their owner and asked in my halting Spanish if they could carry us to El Milagro.

"Claro," he said. "Of course." He rubbed his fingers together in the universal sign of money. "Tres dólares."

"Three dollars," I said to Ann. "I think we should do it."

We rented three—one for each of us to ride and another to carry our backpacks. A barefoot boy, presumably the owner's son, would accompany us on foot; his job, we were told, was to show us the way and bring the horses back once we reached our destination.

My horse wheezed and groaned under my weight as it plodded through mud that often reached to my knees. I felt almost as sorry for that poor animal as I did for myself. But I wasn't about to dismount and attempt to wade through the mud. I hung on with every muscle in my body.

Glancing back, I saw the boy running along a ridge above the horse trail, picking his way through trees and brush and mud, shouting at the horses, and guiding them with a long stick whenever we came to a fork in the trail. I judged him to be about ten years old. Rather than attending school, he was laboring to get us to our destination. The word "privileged" rang in my ears once again.

At one point we were drenched by a downpour like none I had ever before experienced. Although we had plastic ponchos in our backpacks, there was no way to retrieve them in time. We simply resigned ourselves to being soaked.

Late in the afternoon, we arrived at a tattered hand-printed wooden sign nailed to a tree at a lopsided angle: "Bienvenidos al Milagro" (Welcome to the Miracle). Seeing those painted words, battered as they were, I felt relieved;

this horrible journey was about to end. We had reached our destination, the Miracle. I began to regain the enthusiasm I'd felt in Quito.

As soon as I saw the community, my newborn optimism collapsed. I don't know what I'd expected, perhaps a quaint Disneyland type of village, but this was beyond quaint, worse than anything I could have imagined or would have wanted to imagine. A muddy patch of barren earth was bordered by a dozen mud-spattered huts built of rough hand-hewn boards that, like the ones we'd seen earlier, were perpendicular to the ground and looked as if they might disintegrate at any moment. Scrawny dogs barked and snarled at our horses' legs. Naked kids ran up to us, splashing through the mud. They threw stones at the dogs and shouted at me, words I didn't understand.

I stared at Ann. "I think Vietnam might be better."

She gave me a small smile. "Don't kid yourself."

"You can go back home," I said. "I won't hold it against you."

She gave me the finger.

I had the gut-wrenching feeling that we were doomed, prisoners to this land of rain and mud, horrid buses, dirty people and their foul animals. I imagined the jungle was overrun with man-eating snakes, blood-sucking insects, and life-threatening bacteria. Looking back, I'm shamed by my terribly biased perspective. I had no idea, of course, that I would find myself drawn back to this world time and again or that I would come to love this jungle and its people.

I heard a shout from somewhere: "Hola, gringo!"

A man grinning as if he'd found a long-lost relative made his way through the children, hand outstretched. "I'm Professor Mata, the school teacher," he said in Spanish. He wore khaki slacks and a store-bought shirt; both were wrinkled and sweat stained. His smile highlighted a single gold tooth at the front of his mouth and the fact that its neighbor on the right was missing. I would discover that, other than some of his young students, he was one of the few here who spoke Spanish. Everyone else spoke Shuar or Quichua. "Welcome to El Milagro, our little school community." He took our horses' reins and helped us dismount. Pumping my hand, he proclaimed, "You're the agricultural specialist the Peace Corps promised."

"Agricultural specialist?" I dismounted, tumbled off actually, my horse and narrowly escaped falling face first onto the ground. I tried to wipe the mud off my rain-soaked pants. I glanced around at the huddle of people who had assembled to gawk at these strange aliens who had invaded their territory. "I know nothing about agriculture," I said in my lousy Spanish.

"You don't!" He pulled back in surprise. "But that's what we requested."

My intestines turned to water. "Excuse me, Professor. Where's the bathroom?"

"Over there." He pointed toward the woods.

I made a mad dash. Two hand-hewn boards stretched across a stream, with a hole between them. A bunch of leaves was impaled on an overhanging branch. Careful not to slip on the boards that were wet with clumps of brown mush that I wanted to believe was mud, I did what I'd come to do.

When I returned to Professor Mata, he was surrounded by an ever-growing crowd. Ann was pawing through her backpack, looking for something or, more likely, just trying to avoid answering questions. "If you're not an agricultural specialist," Professor Mata asked me, "why are you here?"

To avoid the draft. But, of course I couldn't say that. I stared at Ann.

She abandoned her backpack and came to stand beside me. "Credit and savings," she murmured in English.

I turned back to Professor Mata, tried to show a smile, and stumbled into the Spanish words I recalled learning at the California Peace Corps training camp. "Estoy aquí para formar una cooperativa de crédito y ahorros." (I'm here to help you form a credit and savings cooperative.)

"Credit and savings cooperative?" he replied in Spanish, staring at me in disbelief. "You're joking." He frowned. "You're not joking, are you?"

I shook my head.

He pointed at the huts scattered around us. "What credit? What savings? We have no money. Your papayas for my bananas . . ."

My introduction to US government work: they teach you Spanish and send you to a place where most people speak Shuar or Quichua; they train you for eight weeks in skills nobody will be able to use in the two or more years you are stationed there.

Over the next few days, Ann and I tried to accustom ourselves to life in the jungle. Since the Peace Corps had neglected to arrange a place where we could stay, Professor Mata offered us a tiny room on the bottom floor of his house. Although his house was small, it was the largest and most well-constructed one in the community. Built on the edge of a steep slope, the front of the house and the door looked out to what everyone referred to as "La Plaza"—that muddy patch of earth where we had dismounted our horses and where the children played soccer with a ball made from yarn; it also served as the community's social center. The back of our house was supported by stilts taller than me. Our room had a wooden floor with several missing planks that exposed the muck below. After we became accustomed to the stench from the pigs wallowing beneath, we found those holes convenient places for peeing at night. The only problem was that our cascading urine attracted more pigs. The walls of our room were encrusted with mold but afforded a welcome respite from the prying eyes of curious locals that seemed to follow our every movement. We slept in sleeping bags on the floor. Professor Mata lived above us in a more substantial room that he reached by climbing a ladder. The house was topped with a tin roof that sounded like a thousand drums during the torrents of rain that fell every day and lasted for an hour or so.

As we wandered around this small community, we were struck by the fortitude of the people and by the warmth with which they welcomed us. They knew that we had come to do the impossible, form a credit and savings cooperative. Based on the country's history of exploitation by foreigners and the current conflicts between the Indigenous people and Texaco a hundred miles or so north of us, they had every right to be suspicious of our motives; yet, at one time or another every single person came to us with a smile, shook our hands, and told us his or her name.

Professor Mata fed us twice a day in his upstairs room. His attempts at hospitality at first surprised us, given his disappointment over our lack of agricultural expertise. However, the surprise quickly turned to dismay. Meals almost always consisted of a single fried egg accompanied by fried manioc or plantains on a plate that had been wiped down with a dirty rag. The frying oil was meat based. Black and greasy and reused many times, it rendered the final product something that I found to be most unappetizing. Occasionally, he offered us a bowl of oily soup that included a piece of boney chicken or fish and little noodle-like things that he told us were a special delicacy: grubs pulled out of a rotting tree. Since Amazonian people know that river water is not potable due to the presence of organic matter from fallen trees and dead animals, they drink *chicha*. A kind of beer, it is made by the women who chew pureed manioc roots and spit the liquid into a bowl, allowing it to ferment. During the first week, we drank muddy water laced with foul-tasting iodine tablets from our Peace Corps medical kits. But when these gave out, the only alternative was chicha. Despite our revulsion, we had no choice but to eat and drink these things that were the steady diet of the local people and for which we paid Professor Mata two dollars a week.

Ann and I often returned to the subject of privilege. We were only too aware of the contrast between our lives in the US, which included large, well-furnished houses, grocery stores stocked with hundreds of varieties of different foods, readily available health care, and so many other amenities, and the lives of these people.

El Milagro was not a typical Shuar village. It was, as Professor Mata had said, a "school community" that had been settled by people displaced by overcrowded and impoverished communities in the Andes. They were known as *colonos* (colonists—a word that would later seem significant). "The Shuar don't live in board houses like us," Professor Mata continued. "Theirs are thatched roofed, lots of people crammed together." He shook his head in disgust. "So primitive." Then he added, "Many of the kids here are Shuar. They come to my school to learn Spanish and arithmetic—or because their lands were destroyed by oil companies. Or . . ." he paused, "because their parents were killed in a raid."

"It's true then," I asked, "that the tribal wars continue?"

"Yes, feuds between Shuar clans and against the Achuar that have gone on for generations." He patted my back. "But you don't need to worry, they won't attack us here. We're a school community protected under their own laws."

I had to wonder how strictly those laws were enforced.

Another factor entered my mind at this point. Three centuries of New England Yankees had steeped me in the commandment: "When you're given a job, by God, you do it!" I'd been sent to organize credit and savings cooperatives. It was my job and, despite Professor Mata's warning, I was determined to do it.

The Peace Corps had launched me into the jungle with a backpack filled with comic books that extolled the virtues of credit and savings cooperatives. In color. In Spanish. They were produced by the US Information Service; it was called USIS, although I came to think of it as USELESS.

Each morning, I rose with the sun and handed those comic books to the men, women, and children as they headed into the jungle to cut firewood, gather food and herbal medicines, or hunt. Ann set up a clinic where she used what she'd learned during training about hygiene to teach mothers how to wash their children's cuts and insect bites and treat them with the mercurochrome that was included in our first aid kits.

Every evening, I stood at the center of the community and gave a speech. Between my inept Spanish and the subject—the benefits of credit and savings cooperatives—I had no idea if anything I said was understood by anyone. All I knew was that this was my job.

To my surprise, each night more and more people showed up. Some walked for hours through the jungle and returned to their homes in the black of night—without flashlights. Professor Mata had been wrong. Yankee perseverance was working! Or so I thought.

Then one morning as I headed to the edge of the forest with my pile of comic books, a little girl ran up, touched my arm, and scampered off. A minute or two later she returned to stare at me.

"Why you not dirt?" she asked in halting Spanish.

"What?"

"Dirt." She looked at the sky. "Dirt of star."

"Stardust," I said in English. I didn't know the word in Spanish. "Dirt of star," I parroted back her words.

She nodded. "Yes."

"Why? Me. Dirt of star. Why?"

She glanced toward the forest. "My brother . . ." she indicated a boy standing in the shadows beneath the trees, "said you from there." Her finger pointed up. "I touch you, you turn to dirt—dirt of star." She glanced back to where her brother had been; he was gone. She raced into the forest shouting for him.

I stood there alone, absorbed by the idea that these children thought I'd come from outer space.

Professor Mata walked up to me. "People are confused about you."

I stared at him. "I'm dirt of star."

He nodded.

"But they come to hear my lectures. Credit and savings cooperatives."

"That's your perception." He smiled. "Have you noticed that we don't have radios here? No TVs. There's no electricity." He paused. "No newspapers or magazines either." Another pause. "I'm about the only one who could read them."

It suddenly struck me. "You mean . . ."

"You're the entertainment."

How could I have been so stupid? I now understood that to the children I was a space alien; to the adults, I was the equivalent of a late-night TV comedy show. Every night!

2

AYAHUASCA

ONE MORNING, ANN HEADED OFF to spend a few days with another married couple who were Peace Corps volunteers in a neighboring community. Frequent communications occurred between our communities through foot traffic and these neighbors had sent a message inviting Ann to visit the very successful clinic the wife had set up to help local mothers learn more details about modern hygiene and infant care—a step beyond the cleaning-and-mercurochrome process Ann had already implemented.

A few hours after Ann left, I was suddenly racked with excruciating cramps. I crawled to the hole between the boards in our floor and vomited. Again and again. Then diarrhea. For the rest of the day, I couldn't keep down any food. I could barely stand up. My body shook with chills. I pulled my sleeping bag and backpack next to the hole. I took the medicine provided in the small Peace Corps first-aid kit I carried. I prayed. I meditated. Nothing worked. As the day wore on into the darkest of nights, the vomiting and diarrhea grew worse. In addition to the pain, I was terrified. I barely slept and when I did I awoke soaked in sweat.

The next morning, my empty stomach exploded in violent dry heaves. I was burning up with fever. I desperately searched for a way out. It was a long trek and grueling bus ride to the nearest medical doctor. There was simply no way I could do that. Although Professor Mata brought me hot porridge, I had no desire to eat. I reconciled myself to dying.

Late in the afternoon, Professor Mata led a Shuar man to where I lay in my sleeping bag. Looking at him, I thought I must be delirious. His wrinkled face was covered with frightening black tattoos—a snake slithered from one cheek across his chin to the other cheek, a double-headed spear was etched across his forehead, and lines radiated from his nose like jaguar whiskers. His pearly white teeth were so perfect and contrasted so strongly with Professor Mata's that they seemed unnatural. Naked above the waist, he wore a brown and white striped kilt that hung nearly to his bare feet. His straight black hair fell halfway down his back. In my state of mind, he looked like one of the fierce Indians on the war path I'd read about.

"I'm Entsá, the shaman," he said, as Professor Mata translated.

"Shaman?" It was 1968; I had no idea what that meant.

"Healer," Professor Mata said.

A witch doctor! That was it! Like ones I'd seen in movies who cast evil spells on wagon trains crossing the western plains. He'd come to take revenge on me at my most vulnerable moment for corrupting his people about credit and savings cooperatives. I felt terrified and powerless.

Entsá grasped my hands and pulled me to my feet. I tried to resist but was shaking and weak. Despite the fact that he came only to my shoulders and looked very old, his grip was powerful. Professor Mata held me from behind.

Entsá's coal-black eyes moved up and down my body, scanning me head to toe. He stared so intently into my eyes that he seemed to penetrate my soul. Then he wagged a gnarled finger in my face and murmured something to Professor Mata—who grimaced.

"What did he say?" I asked in a voice so weak I could barely hear myself.

Professor Mata hesitated, then answered quietly, "He said, you're dying."

My body started shaking even more violently than before. "Put me down," I said.

Professor Mata spoke to Entsá. They lowered me back onto my sleeping bag.

Entsá knelt next to me, leaned toward me and muttered something. Professor Mata frowned. "He says dying is good."

It wasn't until later that I learned that the Shuar believe in reincarnation and this shaman thought all my talk about credit and savings cooperatives proved that I was crazy; time to move on. I burst into sobs.

Professor Mata knelt next to Entsá, who spoke to him in a whisper. Professor Mata gave a quick smile, then frowned again and shook his head. They had a long exchange. Even in my feverish state, it sounded like an argument. Finally, Entsá threw up his hands, rose to his feet, and walked away.

Professor Mata watched him go, then turned and looked at me. He said nothing, just stared at me.

"Please," I begged. "What just happened?"

"He told me he could heal you," he said.

"Really?"

"Except, healing you is very dangerous."

Now a jab of fear. "You mean . . . kill me?"

"Oh, no." He paused. "Dangerous for him and me." He stood up and wiped his hands on his pants. "He could heal you and endanger the rest of us."

I felt a twinge of hope and, at the same time, desperation. "Why?"

"This is a mission community." He looked through the open doorway. My eyes followed his to the plaza and across it to the moldy wooden building with the small wooden cross nailed above the door.

A thought came to me. I had to convince him. "Jesus was a healer. He raised Lazarus from the dead."

Professor Mata rubbed the stubble at his chin. "Yes." He glanced down at me. "And was crucified." He walked to the doorway and then came back. "You see, my school is supported by the Catholic church." He dropped to his knees again. "The Church and the Ecuadorian government outlaw the things these shamans do."

I was baffled. "What do the shamans do?"

"They use a plant, a sort of tea. You drink it."

"Poison?"

He shook his head. "It changes you—your mind."

"Like LSD?"

"What's that?"

"Marijuana?"

"That! Never tried it."

"Have you used this plant—the shaman's?"

He glanced furtively around. "I can't talk about it."

"You have, haven't you?" He didn't answer. I was frantic. "Did it help?"

He raised a finger to his lips and nodded.

I pushed myself up from the hard floor. "I want to do it."

Professor Mata muttered something under his breath, crossed himself, and rocked back on his heels. "Maybe," he said. "It could help you, but . . ." He massaged his chin. "But you must promise never to tell anyone."

A twinge of excitement, mixed with hope, ran through me. "Of course."

"Not anyone. Not even your wife."

"I promise."

"If the Church or government finds out that a Shuar shaman did this work on a gringo, they'd put him in prison." He looked up and around. "Or worse." He stared through the open doorway. "And me, too," he whispered. "Maybe you."

"I won't tell a soul," I promised.

After sunset, Professor Mata and a young Shuar man helped me hobble through the jungle to Entsá's home. I felt delirious, but my stomach was empty and the vomiting and dry heaves had stopped.

Entsá's home seemed strangely familiar. It was oval with walls of split-wood staves placed upright in the ground. As we entered, even in my frightened, feeble state I felt a sense of relief. Although the floor was hard-packed dirt, it looked clean, spotless. The arching roof, as tall as three or four men standing on each other's shoulders and constructed of intricately thatched palm leaves, gave the place an open, airy feeling. Spaces between the staves made it possible to see the jungle outside. A smoldering fire near the center sent smoke swirling around us and into the leaves above, and a woman was singing quietly beside the fire.

I was lowered onto a wooden bench. As I peered around, that sensation of familiarity grew even stronger. I was sure that I'd never seen any place like this before, but it felt as though I had. I thought that perhaps the smell of the smoke and fire brought a memory of evenings in front of the fireplace in the New Hampshire cottage where I'd spent my childhood summers. Or perhaps it was the woman's soft voice in the background. Then it hit me. I *had* seen this place before—in the photo shown to me by my seventh-grade history teacher and in films. It resembled the houses in the movie about the book *Northwest Passage*; this place reminded me of ones lived in by the Abnakis in my native New Hampshire during the 1700s.

Professor Mata and the young man picked up the bench with me on it and carried it to a spot near the fire, facing a wooden stool carved to resemble a tortoise. They propped me up against the back of the bench. Professor Mata shoved a blanket against my back to prevent me from falling over.

Out of the misty, smoky darkness, on the far side of the fire, a shadow materialized. Entsá. In the light from the fire, his appearance was more frightening even than before. Wavy red lines drawn across the black tattoos on his face seemed to dance diabolically when he walked toward me. He was naked except for a loincloth, a huge fang that swung from a leather thong across his breast, and a feathered headband. He raised his hands toward me, muttered what sounded like an incantation, turned away, and began to move slowly around the smoldering fire. In the eerie haze, his movements appeared effortless, like those of a jungle cat. Suddenly, he started to shake a rattle and chant in a deep, low voice that was more an animal's growl than anything human.

At first, I fought with the urge to push my weak body off the bench and crawl away. However, I knew that it would be futile. I was too sick. I told myself that if he or Professor Mata wanted me dead, they would simply leave me alone to die. This shaman was my only hope. Then, once again, I experienced that odd sense of having been here before. I forced myself to relax, to accept what was to come.

Entsá seemed immediately to sense my changed mood. He turned toward me. Lifting a burning stick from the fire in one hand, he waved it at me and stepped next to my bench. With his other hand, he shook the rattle so close to my face that I could feel its breeze.

For the first time in two days, I felt a desire to be totally aware of all that was going on around me. I looked for the woman who had been singing, but she was nowhere to be found. I watched carefully as Entsá sat down on the tortoise stool in front of me, continuing to shake the rattle and the burning stick. His chanting grew louder.

Then it stopped. All was silent, except for the high-pitched screeches of tree frogs and insects in the forest outside. Entsá threw the burning stick back into the fire and sat completely still, facing me for what seemed a very long time. With the firelight behind him, I could not see his features, but I felt his eyes on me, as though scanning me as he had that afternoon. Then he set the rattle on the bench beside me, returned to the fire, picked a gourd and cup up from the floor, came back, sat on the stool, and carefully poured the gourd's contents into the cup. He bent over the cup, whispered into it, raised his head to look at me, then blew into the cup.

"Drink." Professor Mata's voice startled me as I felt him lift my hand; the cup touched my fingers.

I leaned forward. As my hand closed around the cup, I started to topple over.

Entsá pushed me back onto the bench. He grabbed my hand, shoved the cup to my mouth, and tilted it.

"Drink," Professor Mata repeated. "All. Now."

It was the foulest thing I'd ever tasted. I choked and gagged.

They both chuckled. Entsá touched my forehead and mumbled something.

"What?"

"Dream," Professor Mata translated. "Touch the jaguar."

"Jaguar?" I glanced around, petrified with fear.

"The jaguar," Professor Mata explained, "is a powerful symbol for the Shuar. If you see it in the visions that are about to come, don't run away. Don't deny your fears. Touch them. Take the jaguar's energy. Let the jaguar guide you to the actions necessary to change you, make you healthy."

Lying there on that bench, the world spun out of control around me. There were flashes of light, but more than anything I felt terribly dizzy. My stomach turned into knots. I wanted to puke but nothing came up. After perhaps half an hour, the dry heaves returned. With a vengeance. The shaman chanted and brushed my body with leaves. Then suddenly things gushed from my mouth. Orange liquid, followed by hideous snakes, disgusting reptilian monsters, and writhing worms that splashed onto the ground and turned into trees.

I know now that I was hallucinating, that Entsá had given me something that in recent years has become popular outside the Amazon but

I'd never heard of then: a tea, made from a couple of plants, called by its Quichua name, ayahuasca.

When the vomiting finally subsided, I lay back on the bench. More images began to flash before me. First, geometric designs and strands of shining florescent beads of lights. These evolved into a boy in New Hampshire. Me! I saw that he was brought up to wash his hands often and to eat sanitized foods from well-washed dishes. After that I saw myself eating a raw egg, greasy plantains, and grub soup off filthy plates and drinking spit beer, *chicha*.

In that trance state, I saw that I ate those foods and drank that beer because that was all there was.

My mother appeared. "This food and drink will kill you," she said. Suddenly, she transformed into a jaguar. The huge cat stood in front of me, baring its teeth and growling.

"Touch the jaguar." Entsá's words echoed through the jungle.

In my vision I stepped toward the jaguar, reached out and touched it. It dissolved and I saw Shuar men and women. They were healthy, robust. Among them were elders. A voice spoke. "Many of us live to be very old. Our foods are fresh and healthy and make us strong. We drink chicha because it purifies the river water."

The shaman stopped chanting. The only sounds were those from the dark jungle—tree frogs, bats, insects, and night birds. I fell into a deep sleep.

When I woke up, the sun was shining. To my surprise I had no cramps. No nausea, fever, or diarrhea. I was hungry. As I lay there on that bench, I understood that it was not the food and drink that had been killing me; it was my mind-set, my perception that the food and drink would kill me. I'd fallen into a perception trap. Recognizing that, I felt like a new person. I peered through the spaces between the upright staves at the forest outside. It looked greener than before and less hostile. I took a deep breath. The air smelled fresher. I was struck by the thought that my fear of the food and drink and of the jungle itself was really the fear I had of things different, the unfamiliar, the unknown. I had spent much of my life afraid of change.

Entsá and Professor Mata came and stood beside me. "You've recovered," Entsá said in Spanish and smiled sweetly.

When I thanked him, he held up a thick piece of vine, about as long as his arm. "This healed you," he said. "Ayahuasca. You shapeshifted from dying to living."

The three of us walked outside. I spread my arms to the jungle and gave a loud shout of thanks. I felt liberated.

Entsá patted me on the back. "Good," he said and then went on to tell me in halting Spanish—with, now and then, help from Professor Mata—that before my arrival in his community, he had been visited by what he called *Los Sabios*—Wise Ones—who came out of the sky in blue globes.

"You mean extraterrestrials, from other stars?" I asked.

"Once shamans," he said. "They shapeshift. Smarter than us. Travel to other stars, yes. But not in metal tubes like airplanes. They do it through . . ." He pointed at his head and then his heart and gave a guttural laugh. He said that they had told him that people in lands far away who were destroying the earth would send him a student. He explained that the Shuar saw my people and our oil companies as the thing they most feared; it was his job to confront those fears and to take actions that would keep the oil companies away. He'd waited for someone like me. "You'll be a shaman," he said. "So you can change your people." He smiled. "You'll be my first gringo student."

I had graduated from business school and, in those days, there was no future in shamanism; but because Entsá had saved my life, I felt obligated to acquiesce. Besides, he and his plant had accomplished the seemingly impossible. I was intrigued by the idea of delving deeper into the mysteries of whatever it was they had done.

Professor Mata explained to Entsá that it would have to be a secret apprenticeship. "No one," he said. "Not even his wife can know." The shaman smiled and nodded enthusiastically.

Ann returned late that afternoon. We hugged and talked about how much we'd missed each other; she had no inkling of what I'd been through, and I kept my promise not to tell her. Filled with enthusiasm over the infant-care project the other volunteer had started, she told me she was going to replicate it.

Professor Mata took it upon himself to help both of us improve our Spanish. He engaged us in lengthy conversations throughout the day. The fact that Entsá spoke more Spanish than he'd originally let on motivated me to improve mine.

Professor Mata also helped me keep my shamanic training a secret from Ann. He organized her infant-care clinics around the times I spent with Entsá. Looking back, I can see that this was the beginning of a deceptive life that would continue throughout my years as an EHM. During the next months, while Ann worked with mothers and their infants, I sneaked off to learn about shamanism from Entsá.

After about the third month, Entsá informed me that he was going to plant what he called "tsentsak" (invisible darts modeled after the real darts the Shuar used in their blowguns) into my heart. He cupped his hands over my left wrist and blew. Crazy as it seemed, I felt something enter my wrist and quickly move up my arm, into my heart. He told me that when I returned to the US, I could blow these into people who needed healing or situations that needed to be changed and I'd receive answers about what I could do to facilitate the necessary changes.

From these clandestine meetings with Entsá, I developed an intellectual interest in shamanism. Once a month, Ann and I were obliged to check in at the regional Peace Corps office in Cuenca to prove that we were still alive. I say "obligated," but in fact, we relished meeting with other volunteers, feasting on steaks and french fries, and drinking real beer and potable water. In retrospect, I see that it was one more of the privileges we enjoyed that were not available to the people of El Milagro or most other Ecuadorians at the time.

The Peace Corps office had an extensive English-language library where I found books like *At Play in the Fields of the Lord* by Peter Matthiessen and articles such as "The Sound of Rushing Water" by Michael Harner that helped me understand the ayahuasca I'd taken and the principles behind shamanism.

I wondered whether anything besides my preconditioned mind had caused that illness. Laboratory tests required by the Peace Corps while we were in Cuenca indicated that at some point I'd contracted parasites. Had that been the underlying cause? Years later, I would read that ayahuasca can help rid the body of parasites through the alkaloids it contains.[1] Although I'm not sure exactly what happened that night, I do know that after taking the ayahuasca I had a very different attitude toward the foods I was eating and the chicha I was drinking and that my health improved.

The more I worked with Entsá, the more I came to appreciate that "touching the jaguar" meant recognizing that human reality is molded by our perceptions and that to change ourselves or our world, we must break through the barriers that imprison us in old ways of thinking and acting. If we run from, or deny, our fears, they will hound us. By confronting them, we take their power. The word Entsá used was "Arutam." In Shuar it describes the ability to transform, to shapeshift.

3

FIGHTING COMMUNISM

A FEW DAYS AFTER my ayahuasca experience, three male Peace Corps volunteers arrived in our community. They led mules stacked with surveying equipment, construction tools, and sacks of bulgur flour, corn, and grass seeds. Greeting them enthusiastically, Professor Mata instructed them to stockpile these things in a shed next door to his house.

As those three volunteers, Professor Mata, Ann, and I sat together that evening eating a dinner of sandwiches they'd brought from Cuenca, I understood the real reason why we'd been assigned to this community.

At the request of the US Agency for International Development (USAID), the Peace Corps had become the spearhead for a program aimed at relocating poor Andean people to the jungle. The justification was that these people were ripe pickings for what Washington, DC, claimed was an intense campaign by Castro's Cuba to spread communism throughout Latin America. The propaganda machines warned that the Soviets, through their support for Cuba, would soon dominate Latin America. The US would be next. Che Guevara, who was part of Castro's revolutionary forces, had been captured in a CIA-directed operation and executed in Bolivia less than a year before our arrival in Ecuador. Che's presence so far from Cuba was offered as proof that Cuba was intent on dominating the continent. The American media warned that the "red wave" of communism was about to inundate cities and villages throughout the Andes. The solution was to transport poor people from these Andean regions deep into the Amazon. This, it was theorized, would take them out of areas that were considered potential hotbeds for revolution and into remote forests where they might make a living and where they would pose less of a threat to the US-supported government.

USAID helped Ecuador craft a program modeled after the 1862 US Homestead Act. Land would be deeded to anyone who cut down a section of pristine rain forest and made it "productive"—which meant planting it in grass and raising cattle. The three Peace Corps volunteers were part of this program. They had been trained as community organizers and surveyors. The area selected for colonization was a two-day trek beyond El Milagro.

Now I understood that the reason Ann and I had been stationed in El Milagro was to guard the equipment and supplies that supported this operation.

I would later see that this colonization project was part of a much larger strategy to colonize all of Latin America, to dominate its resources and people, and to create a belief system, a perception, that the US, not Soviet-supported Cuba, offered the answer to the problems that plagued its southern neighbors.

Although Professor Mata was happy to receive payment from the US government to supervise the flow of goods, he let Ann and me know that the colonization program was doomed to fail. There were, he said, two huge problems. First, the entire concept was based on the deduction made by US officials who flew over the jungle in small planes that large tracks of forest were uninhabited. Second, these officials believed that, like the American Great Plains, the land beneath the trees was fertile.

"Both assumptions are false," he told us. "The Shuar are hunters and gatherers who need large areas of forest in order to survive; to them the land is not uninhabited."

He led us along a trail into the trees just outside the community, knelt down, and jabbed a finger into the ground. "Look here. You can see that the rain forest has extremely thin topsoil—next to deserts, the worst in the world. The topsoil is generated by falling leaves, dying trees, and the mushrooms and microorganisms that convert them to earth; once cleared, the soil washes away during the rains. The sun kills the mushrooms and microorganisms and bakes the clay-like soil as hard as bricks."

He went on to explain that to further complicate matters, aggressive land speculators from the Ecuadorian coast were claiming homesteader rights and moving deeper and deeper into Shuar Territory. Skirmishes had erupted. "A few days before you arrived," he continued, "one of these, a guy named Rodrigo Ulloa, was carried here by his brother and a couple friends on a stretcher they'd made. He'd been hiding behind a log ready to ambush a group of Shuar when a bushmaster snake slithered up and bit him. He was dead by the time I saw him."

He took hold of my arm and looked into my eyes. "You must tell your bosses that this foolishness, this colonization program, must stop."

"What about the money you receive?"

"To hell with it. My community, my school, is caught in the middle." He spread his arms toward the forest around us. "If this craziness, this destruction, and the fighting continue, we're doomed." He covered his eyes and moaned. "Please write letters," he said, lowering his hands, "to the Peace Corps, USAID, the embassy, the president of the United States . . . tell them that colonization won't work here, the Shuar claim these lands as theirs, and the soil is no good for farming." He locked the fingers of his hands together, like he was praying, and raised them to us. "Please insist. This must stop."

I did most of what he requested. I wrote letters to the head of the Peace Corps in Ecuador and the director in Washington and to USAID and embassy offices in Quito and mailed them the next time we were in Cuenca. I stopped short of writing to President Johnson. In those letters, I detailed all the problems with the colonization program, including the fact that Amazon forest soils had nothing in common with those of the US Great Plains and therefore the US Homestead Act had no bearing. In addition, Professor Mata and I both talked to the volunteers who came through.

No one wanted to hear what we had to say. US officials in Quito and Washington had staked their careers on this program. The Peace Corps volunteers depended on it to keep them from being drafted and they believed in colonization. It was one more lesson in my evolving education about US government work and the way we abuse our privileges.

Instead of stopping the program, the Peace Corps took a very different approach. In 1970, in an obvious move to shut us up, it transferred Ann and me out of the rain forest and back to Cuenca. I was assigned to help a group of impoverished *campesino* brickmakers high in the Andes form a marketing cooperative, while Ann was given the job of training handicapped people to work in Cuenca businesses. Although I was sad to leave Entsá and my training behind, Ann and I were excited about moving into a tiny apartment that had a real toilet in a city of nearly one hundred thousand residents. In addition to an assortment of small stores, Cuenca offered restaurants and three theaters that featured American movies with Spanish subtitles. "I think I've seen enough mud for a lifetime," Ann quipped as we scraped the grime off our backpacks and sleeping bags one afternoon.

PART 2

The Death Economy

1970–1987

*It was a system that was bound to fail,
to kill itself—what economists would
later define as a Death Economy.*

4

MORE SECRETS

THE BRICKMAKERS that the Peace Corps wanted me to help lived in Sinincay, an area that was only a few hundred miles, as the crow flies, from Shuar Territory and yet looked as if it were more closely related to the moon than to the rain forests. At an altitude of around ten thousand feet, it was barren, arid, and forbidding. The primary language, Quichua, dates back to pre-Incan times. Typical of Quichua speakers in 1970, the brickmakers were poor; exploited; plagued by disease, hunger, and high infant mortality rates; and excluded from most economic sectors and social circles outside their own.

Their one valuable resource was clay. Men and boys dug it from the ground. Women and girls molded it into bricks, which they laid out in long rows on the hard earth. After sun drying, the bricks were hauled on the backs of men to the tops of huge wood-fired ovens and handed down, bucket brigade fashion, to be stacked inside. When the firing process was completed, the bricks were sold to businessmen who owned trucks and warehouses in Cuenca. These men grew rich by buying cheap and selling at huge profits to final users: architects, engineers, and other members of the wealthy elite who were known as the *buena gente* (good people). It was truly a medieval system that handsomely benefited everyone except those whose hard work had fabricated the bricks.

My job was to help the brickmakers organize a marketing cooperative that could rent its own truck and warehouse in Cuenca, do away with the middlemen, and return the profits to the brickmakers and their families.

It seemed like a straightforward assignment. However, I soon discovered that it was much more difficult than I'd expected. It required that the people of Sinincay change their thinking about how they related to the world and to the buena gente, people they had been told for decades were superior to them in every way. They had to change their perceptions to change the reality of the way they conducted business and their lives.

It was especially important that I teach the man who had been elected by the co-op members to run the warehouse we rented in Cuenca, Don José Quischpe, about accounting, inventory control, and other basic management tools. He had to be convinced that, despite the fact that he had completed only the equivalent of fourth grade, he could do what he had previously believed required an advanced education and that he was smart enough and strong enough to negotiate deals with architects and engineers.

Although none of this was easy, I have to say that I felt relieved to finally have a job that actually made sense. I was no longer trying to convince people without money to form a credit and savings co-op or promote the destructive colonization of the rain forest. In a way, I was using things I'd learned from Entsá to help people understand that their perception of themselves and others could change, could shapeshift. When Don José and a couple of other key members finally got it, reality changed for the entire community.

During this time, once again, I was very aware of my privileged status. The brickmakers spent long hours every day doing back-breaking work and then, in the cold Andean night, returned to crude adobe homes with no electricity or running water. I spent most of my days at a desk in the Cuenca warehouse and my nights in a tiny but cozy Cuenca apartment with Ann and modern amenities. I also knew that in a year I would return to all the advantages of a white, educated male in the United States, while the brickmakers would continue their lives in the barren mountains of Sinincay.

One afternoon, upon arriving at the warehouse, I was informed that Don José was extremely sick and being healed by a shaman. I hopped on a bus to Sinincay. When I arrived there, I told Don José's teenage son, Antonio, that I'd trained with a Shuar shaman and asked to observe the healing. He motioned for me to follow him into a small adobe hut.

A dozen or so people sat huddled about Don José, who was stand-ing, nearly naked, in the center of the room. His son pointed at a woman slowly circling him, brushing him with bundles of plants she held in both hands and chanting.

"Maria," Antonio said, bowing toward her in a sign of respect. "The shaman."

She was wearing a white blouse embroidered with delicate flowers, a navy-blue skirt that reached to her ankles, and open-toed sandals. Her long black hair was pulled back in a loose bun. At one point, she glanced at Antonio and me and smiled. Her face was wrinkled like that of an elderly woman, but given the energy involved in the work she was doing, she seemed ageless. Eventually, she shifted from the plants to a couple of palm-sized rocks that she gently rubbed across Don José's head, chest, and belly. Most surprising of all to me was that she ended by sipping a liquid from a bottle and then blowing it on him in a very fine sweet-smelling mist.

When the healing was over, Don José stepped through the group of people to welcome me. He was beaming and did not appear at all sick. I had to wonder whether there was something else going on here; perhaps he had just given himself a day off to perform this ritual.

"How are you?" I asked as he pumped my hand.

"I was very sick," he answered. "Fever, nausea, and headache. But now," he smiled, "I feel great." He called to the shaman. She came and stood beside him. "This is Maria Quischpe."

Despite the wrinkles, her face radiated youthful joy. "I love my work," she said when her hand grasped mine. Her fingers vibrated with energy.

Looking into her sparkling eyes, I immediately had the desire to spend more time with her and learn from her as a teacher. "You are the shaman. Are you also Don José's relative?"

"No," she giggled, showing a couple of gold teeth surrounded by very white ones. "Quischpe is a common name among us."

Without giving it a second thought, I blurted out that I had appren-ticed with a Shuar shaman and would like to learn more about Quechua shamanism.

"You may have heard the Prophecy of the Eagle and the Condor?" I shook my head. "Well, there'll be another opportunity for that. Briefly, it says that it's time for all people, all cultures, to share our knowledge." She gave a slight bow of her head. "I'd be delighted to exchange teachings with you."

It was the beginning of a relationship that would affect me deeply. Don José, like Professor Mata, let me know that I'd have to keep all this secret. "The Catholic priest who lives here has big power and he hates shamans," he explained. "Please, not a word to anyone."

I agreed, and—like my earlier agreement about Entsá—I understand now that this was another step forward into a secret life. By honoring my promises to Professor Mata and Don José not to mention my shamanic interests to anyone, including Ann, I'd headed down a path that would be habituated for years. In addition to the many ways secrecy affected me, it ultimately destroyed my marriage.

But in those days, Ann was happy with her project to help Cuenca's handicapped. She quickly struck up a relationship with the chamber of commerce, a group of key businessmen, including several Jewish industrialists who'd fled Nazi Germany and welcomed her ideas about hiring men and women who had lost their sight or an arm or leg, as long as she was willing to personally train them. The job appealed to Ann's compassionate nature and she also found it relatively easy to master and teach the tasks necessary for disabled people to earn an income—many for the first time in their lives.

Over the next months, though most of my job restricted me to the Cuenca warehouse, I tried to make it to Sinincay at least once every two weeks. When there, I spent as much time as possible with Maria. She took a deep interest in learning about Entsá and his methods. In exchange, she taught me her healing practices. She had her patients rub unlit white candles over their bodies: then she lit them and read in the "auras" of the candles areas that needed healing. After that, she shook raw eggs around her patients to drain off negative energies, massaged their bodies with bundled branches from stinging nettles and other plants to stimulate the flow of blood and positive energies. She used stones she had gathered from the slopes of volcanoes to focus healing energies on the areas shown by the candles as needing it. Finally, she filled her mouth with that sweet-smelling liquid that she told me she had produced from high-altitude wildflowers and sprayed it over them, head to toe, front, back, and sides.

"The most important thing," she said, "is to alter the energetic spirits of the patient." When she saw my look of confusion, she laughed. "What you might call the dream of the patient."

I described the way Entsá had healed me and asked if she had ever used ayahuasca.

"No," she replied. "Plant energy, plant spirit is wonderful, but often the ones like ayahuasca aren't available here in the mountains. So why rely on them?" She smiled. "I could've healed you without that plant. Like your Shuar friends, we know that the dream is everything. The way we live is determined by the way we see ourselves and our relationship to the world around us."

Entsá had introduced me to something that would mold the rest of my life. Maria had confirmed it. In the years to come, I would learn that shamans from different cultures—in Africa, Asia, the Middle East, and Latin America—share a common belief, one expressed by the title of a book I would write many years after leaving the Peace Corps: *The World Is As You Dream It*. This same belief is part of the Prophecy of the Eagle and the Condor that Maria had referred to, as well as the Mayan Prophecy of 2012 and others that I would later learn and teach.

I would come to appreciate the amazing power we have to alter human actions by changing our perceptions. I would see that this power can be applied on many levels: individual, communal, national, and global. I would understand that perception and the resulting actions drive everything that is impacted by humans—which increasingly translates to everything on our planet, including our social-governmental-economic systems. These ideas that first germinated in Ecuador would provide the foundations for the books I would write and the organizations and movements I would support later in my life.

5

ECONOMIC HIT MAN

DURING MY LAST YEAR as a Peace Corps volunteer in Ecuador, I was visited by Einar Greve, a vice president of Chas. T. Main (MAIN), an international consulting firm that kept a very low profile and worked primarily for the US and other governments and international development organizations, like USAID and the World Bank. Einar told me that he was in charge of studies to determine whether Ecuador qualified for billions of dollars in World Bank loans to build hydroelectric dams.

Beginning with that first meeting, Einar described the benefits of working for a company like MAIN. When I mentioned that I had been accepted by the National Security Agency before joining the Peace Corps and that I was considering going back to them, he informed me that he was a colonel in the US Army Reserve and sometimes acted as an NSA liaison. He gave me the impression that part of his assignment in Ecuador was to recruit me or at least evaluate my capabilities. I had a feeling that Uncle Frank was looking over Einar's shoulder at me.

Einar and I spent several days together, and after he left, we communicated by mail. At his request, I sent him reports assessing Ecuador's economic prospects and the attitudes of its people toward the US. When my Peace Corps tour was over, in early 1971 he invited me to a job interview at MAIN's headquarters in Boston.

I met with the company's president and its chairman of the board and had dinner with several vice presidents. They impressed upon me that MAIN's work helped poor people around the world rise out of poverty and improve their standards of living. They showed me economic studies indicating that when lots of money is invested in infrastructure, a country's economy grows. All this was very consistent with what I'd learned in business school; it convinced me that MAIN's projects were extremely beneficial. After a couple of days of being treated like a star athlete who is wooed by professional teams, I was offered a salary that was beyond my imagination, more than three times what my dad made as a teacher. In January 1971, the month I turned twenty-six, the age when the Vietnam draft no longer wanted me, I became an economist at MAIN.

Deeply motivated by what I saw as the company's commitment to helping the poor, I worked very hard to apply myself to this new job. It took me to assignments in Asia, Latin America, and the Middle East. In less than two years I replaced the chief economist who was fired because he could not handle the challenges of working in these countries. As the new chief economist, I proceeded to build a staff of more than three dozen highly qualified experts and was made the youngest partner in the firm's one hundred–year history. It took me several more years to see through the veneer of "doing good." However, eventually I realized that what I was really doing was using fancy economic studies to convince leaders of countries around the globe with resources US corporations wanted, like oil, to accept huge loans from the World Bank, the Inter-American Development Bank, the Asian Development Bank, or one of their sister organizations. The funds would be used to hire US engineering companies to build infrastructure projects. The loans would leave the countries wallowing in debt. To pay them off, the country would be forced to sell its oil or other resources cheap to our corporations or meet other "conditionalities" that served the interests of what was becoming an American empire. I and others with similar jobs began to joke among ourselves about being "economic hit men," EHMs.

Our job involved offering country leaders huge "rewards" for cooperating. A president's son-in-law who owned a company that leased construction equipment would receive an extremely lucrative contract (e.g., millions of dollars for equipment worth half that amount). A sister's catering service would provide all the food to construction crews at greatly inflated prices. The children of the country's leaders and their friends would be admitted to US colleges with full scholarships and promises of good jobs during school vacations and following graduation. These and many other perks were outright bribes and yet totally legal.

If the leaders balked at our deals, we reminded them of those who had previously refused and were overthrown in coups or were assassinated: Iran's Premier Mossadegh, Chile's President Allende, Guatemala's President Arbenz, the Congo's President Lumumba, Vietnam's President Diem, and a long list of ministers of state, judges, and lower-level officials. We EHMs made sure that country leaders knew that people we called "jackals"—highly skilled hit men and women with talents very different from ours who often worked as CIA contractors—were right behind us. We didn't pack guns, but they did.

Once the leaders were convinced, their nations became our pawns. A country assumed the debt, but it never saw a penny of the money. Those funds were used to hire US engineering companies, like Bechtel, Halliburton, Stone and Webster, and MAIN, to build electric power systems, highways, ports, industrial parks, and other infrastructure projects in the countries. The funds were transferred from a bank in Washington, DC, to the company's bank in Houston, San Francisco, New York, or Boston. Although some of the people in the top executive offices of the World Bank and its sisters, as well as those in the engineering companies, understood that it was a shell game, most of their subordinates—engineers, economists, and others—did not. They were simply doing the jobs they'd been educated and trained to do.

The big winners were the US corporations that built the projects and those that benefited from the improved infrastructure—ones that drilled for oil, mined for gold and other minerals, or employed cheap labor in sweatshops—both types profited handsomely. The second tier of winners were the wealthy and powerful local families; their businesses also flourished due to the improved infrastructure. However, the majority of the country's people suffered because funds were diverted from education, health care, and other social services to make interest payments on the loans.

In the end, the countries were never able to pay off the principle. This was an integral part of the EHM strategy. Teaming up with the International Monetary Fund (IMF), we forced the countries to restructure the loans and sell their oil and other resources cheap to our corporations without environmental or social regulations. We convinced them to privatize their utilities, prisons, schools, and other public-sector businesses and turn them over to US investors. In some cases, we coerced them into voting with Washington against Cuba or another country in the UN or allowing the Pentagon to build military bases on their soil.

During the early years at my job, I had found it easy to convince myself that I was doing the right thing.

South Vietnam had fallen to the Communist north, and now, I told myself, all of us were threatened by the Soviet Union and China. Indonesia would go next, then the "red tide" of communism would sweep across Asia, Latin America, Africa, and Europe and into the US. I was told that I was on the forefront of defending the entire globe against a menace worse than Hitler.

I'd been taught in business school that improved infrastructure stimulates economic growth and that prosperity would persuade nations everywhere to choose the US form of capitalism and democracy over communism. Our sophisticated econometric models showed that a country's economy would mushroom—and everyone would be better off—as a result of our projects. Statistics indicated that more and more people were being connected to electricity and water and sewerage and were buying TVs and other consumer goods.

Then, over time, I began to see that the econometric models and statistics were skewed in favor of the rich. In the countries where I worked (and most of the world), a few families owned 70 to 95 percent of the recorded assets; their financial interests composed most, if not all, of the GDP. The rest of the population was part of a subeconomy that never made the statistics. The rich were getting richer while the poor were staying the same or becoming poorer and many in the middle class were becoming impoverished. Statistically, the economy was growing, yet that growth only benefited an extremely small percentage of the population. The gap between rich and poor was widening drastically.

Even as I came to understand the biases in the models, it never occurred to me at the time that this inequality would eventually generate deep unrest, disillusionment, and violence. Ultimately it would lead to such desperation that millions of people would become homeless

migrants or turn to drugs, suicide, or acts of violence that would be classified as terrorism by their victims and patriotism by their supporters.

It also never occurred to me that this whole system was ultimately
self-destructive. The big corporations were sucking resources from countries around the planet at an unsustainable rate. The driving goal of the
corporations was to maximize short-term profits. CEOs were intent on
increasing short-term stock prices, market share, or both without regard
for the future. It was a system that was bound to fail, to kill itself—what
economists would later define as a Death Economy. At the time, we were
unaware that fossil fuel and other emissions, along with chemical fer-
tilizers and insecticides, were polluting our atmosphere, poisoning our
waters, and destroying our soils. It was a social-governmental-economic
system that was totally irrational—truly a Death Economy.

Looking back, I can thank my Peace Corps experience for helping me
understand the fallacy of the studies and the econometric models we
produced, although not the intricacies of the larger problems. My time in
Ecuador had offered me a different perspective from that of other EHMs
and the bankers and engineers who remained blind to the reality of what
was happening. I'd been on the other side, lived with the people down-
stream from the dams who suffered from the loss of water and fishing
and aquatic activities and with the ones who ended up prostituting themselves to oil companies and sweatshops.

My EHM job was a case of molding reality through changing perceptions—a technologically sophisticated form of proselytization. We produced mathematical models and propagandistic reports that were used
to create a story that life would improve for everyone as a result of the
massive loans. We marketed this story to ourselves, US taxpayers, and
the leaders of the countries with resources our corporations wanted.
Those leaders then passed the story on to their citizens. Our message was
that we were doing good around the world, but the truth was that we were
spreading corporate colonialism and building a global empire.

Once I began to understand this, I tried to deny it. Ann and I were
living what I thought was the American dream in Boston. I often traveled
first class to places I'd previously only fantasized about, stayed in the best
hotels, and ate in the finest restaurants. I had my own offices in Colombia,

Indonesia, Iran, and Panama, as well as at MAIN's Boston headquarters, and I oversaw projects in many other countries. I didn't want to give up that life. I hung out with people who supported the system, who kept saying that we were doing the right thing. I wanted to hear this; I craved confirmation that I could continue making a great salary and seeing the world.

However, deep down, I was miserable. I drank heavily. I slept with women I barely knew. I anesthetized myself with Valium. I was haunted by nightmares. In the mornings, I'd force myself awake with overdoses of caffeine. I justified this with excuses about jet lag, but in my heart, I knew the truth: I was depressed; I hated myself.

Ann and I quarreled constantly. She complained that I had changed, that I was not the man she'd married or with whom she had shared those Peace Corps years. One night she asked me if there were other women in my life. I flew into a rage, stomped out of our Boston apartment, and spent the night in a hotel. But the next day, I admitted that I'd had a number of affairs. It was the beginning of the end of our marriage.

I was trapped in the trance of a materialistic system that was devouring itself. I had grown up feeling poor, surrounded by rich boys in a New Hampshire boarding school. Yet here I was, before my thirtieth birthday, living a life of luxury and meeting with important people. I had it made. How could I even consider getting out?

Something else also kept me in. As I traveled to places in Asia, Latin America, and the Middle East, I'd take as much time off as I could to study with shamans. Because of my experiences in Ecuador and then other countries, I understood how to ingratiate myself to shamans from a number of cultures, participate in their ceremonies, and learn more about their approaches. During the 1970s I spent a lot of time with a Mayan shaman in Mexico's Yucatán Peninsula, Viejo Itza. He taught me the Mayan Prophecy of 2012 long before Hollywood and a number of writers incorrectly interpreted it as a doomsday prophecy—as explained later in this book.

I told no one about this other life I was leading as a student of shamanism. The people at MAIN, the World Bank, the IMF, and the governments and other institutions I dealt with would have thought me crazy. I'd have been fired. Although shamanism is widely accepted these days, back then it was not.

The tension between Ann and me had continually mounted. We separated several times, moving into individual apartments, got back together, and then in 1979, after consulting with a lawyer and agreeing on how to share our assets, Ann flew to the Dominican Republic and filed for a quick divorce. I moved out of our plush twenty-sixth-floor penthouse overlooking Boston Common and onto a sailboat in Boston Harbor.

The nightmares that had begun before our divorce intensified. In a recurring one, I stood before the president of a Latin American country, holding a wad of money outstretched in one hand and a gun behind my back in the other. "You and your friends," I said as I offered him the money, "can get very rich, or . . ." I waved the gun in his face, "I'll call in the jackals." Then I aimed the gun at my own head and shot myself.

My conscience, my upbringing—every fiber in my body screamed at me to get out. On the other hand, everything I'd learned in business school told me to stay in. As did my peers. I was living in a world I'd dreamed for myself and I convinced myself that this was indeed the American dream.

Then, during one of my trips to Panama, I began a relationship with a young woman who'd become a prostitute. It was the only way she knew to support herself and a baby conceived with a man who, she had thought, loved her and then disappeared. She was a mirror to me. I too was a prostitute. When I peered into that mirror I had to admit that although the life she'd been forced into was, unlike mine, terribly difficult and degrading, my own prostitution did damage on a far larger scale. I was corrupting and threatening heads of state. I was hurting millions of people. I was part of a deceptive scheme that was taking the US, the world—and me—into a very dark place.

In another nightmare, I tumbled down a black tunnel that echoed with the screams of tortured souls and I saw images of sailing ships filled with shackled, dying slaves. I woke up staring at two empty bottles on my bedside table: one contained Valium, the other rum. I picked up the rum bottle. As I turned it over in my hands, the words of a song I'd sung as a boy came to me.

Fifteen men on a dead man's chest
Yo ho ho and a bottle of rum
Drink and the devil had done the rest
Yo ho ho and a bottle of rum.

I heard the refrain: *John, the devil has taken you.*

The evening after that dream, I took myself into a shamanic journey. I sat in a favorite chair, turned on a recording of a flutist playing Andean music, and envisioned myself lying on a bed of moss in the New Hampshire woods I'd loved as a child. This was what I referred to as my "sacred place," a place where I felt totally safe and secure—and a technique I'd later teach in workshops. I called on Entsá and Maria to help me. Maria massaged me with plants and sacred stones and sprayed me with flower water. Entsá touched my left wrist with one hand and my heart with the other, reminding me of the invisible darts he'd blown into me. "These can heal you," he advised. He smiled and added, "Use them to shapeshift the situation you helped create that is threatening the world as we know it."

"How do I start?" I asked.

He answered, "Touch your jaguar."

Immediately, as I sat in that chair listening to the flute, I saw an image of the building in Boston's Prudential Center where MAIN's offices were located. When I touched the jaguar, it turned into a sailboat anchored in the cove of a tropical island.

Soon after that, in March 1980, I rented a sailboat in the Virgin Islands. I anchored it late one afternoon in a cove off St. John Island that was very similar to the one I had visualized, rowed the dinghy ashore, and struggled up a steep hill to the crumbling ruins of an ancient sugar plantation. I sat there with a can of beer and watched the sun sink into the Caribbean. It all seemed very idyllic. Suddenly a thought struck me: This plantation had witnessed untold misery; hundreds of African slaves had died here—forced at gunpoint and under the sharp bite of whips to work for the wealthy owners. The tranquility of the place masked its history of brutality. In that moment, I realized that I was an heir of those earlier slavers. Mine had been a more modern approach, subtler—I'd never had to see the dying bodies or hear the screams of agony. But, because I could cut myself off from those personal aspects, the bodies and the screams, perhaps in the final analysis I was the greater sinner.

Furious with myself, I stood up, grabbed a large stick, and beat it against the stone wall near me. Then I sat down, calmed myself, and placed my left hand and wrist over my heart. In the beat of my heart I could feel those invisible darts palpitating. I knew then what I had to do. I returned to my office in Boston and on April 1, 1980, I quit.

I was relieved to be out of that horrible system when, about a year later, two of my former clients died in what the world was convinced were CIA-orchestrated assassinations. The news shocked, saddened, and angered me. I knew the facts and stories behind the events that lead to the deaths of Ecuador's president Jaime Roldós and Panama's head of state Omar Torrijos.

6

JACKALS STRIKE

JAIME ROLDÓS WAS A POPULIST LAWYER and a nationalist who, when he campaigned for the presidency of Ecuador in 1978, captured international attention by going after the oil companies and the system that supported them.

The oil companies had a long and reprehensible history in Ecuador. During World War II, Standard Oil, which had been founded by John D. Rockefeller, won an auction to develop oil in Peru. At a similar Ecuadorian auction, Royal Dutch Shell beat out Standard Oil. John D. Rockefeller's son, Nelson, was President Franklin Roosevelt's coordinator of inter-American affairs. An avid promoter of Standard Oil's Amazonian interests, he was upset over the outcome of the Ecuadorian auction. After Hitler invaded Holland, Nelson Rockefeller convinced the US government and its allies that a "Nazi company" should not control so much of the hemisphere's petroleum (he neglected to point out that Germany could not transport oil through the American-controlled Panama Canal or Amazon River). At a 1942 summit, the Rio Protocol was signed by the hemisphere's most powerful countries; it forced Ecuador to transfer about 40 percent of its territory to Peru. The oil rights went to Standard Oil and, later, Texaco.

By the time Jaime Roldós's campaign got underway, Texaco was extracting a lot of oil from the greatly reduced amount of land Ecuador still held in the Amazon basin. In his speeches, Roldós promised that revenues from oil would raise the income levels of Ecuador's poor. At a time of very strong right-wing movements and brutal dictators in Ecuador and much of Latin America, Roldós advocated for human rights and major social reforms.

In 1979 Jaime Roldós became Ecuador's first democratically elected president to follow a long line of US-supported dictators. Honoring his campaign promises, he insisted that Texaco and other oil companies pay Ecuadorians a fair share of the profits they gained from Ecuadorian oil. Texaco adamantly opposed any laws that might set new precedents—not only in Ecuador but also in other countries.

I, and other EHMs, were dispatched to Ecuador to convince the president to change his ways. President Roldós was offered the opportunity to become personally wealthy and gain the full support of the US government, including the CIA. He refused.

The oil companies and Washington pulled out all the stops. Their public relations people launched an international campaign to vilify President Roldós, their lobbyists swept into Quito and Washington, and their pundits hit the TV circuits. They painted this democratically elected president—who favored social reform but not communism—as a Soviet puppet.

President Roldós refused to cave in to bribes and intimidation. Instead, his speeches warned Big Oil and all foreign interests that unless they implemented plans that would help Ecuador's people, they would have to leave his country. On May 24, 1981, he delivered a major speech in Quito and then headed off to a community in southern Ecuador on board his private airplane. The flight ended in a ball of fire, killing him, his wife, several members of his staff, a flight attendant, and the two pilots.

The world was stunned. Ecuadorians and people throughout Latin America were outraged. Newspapers condemned the crash as a CIA assassination. In addition to the knowledge that Washington and the oil companies openly hated him, concrete evidence supported the assassination allegations, including engineering tests conducted on the plane's two engines in Switzerland and the fact that the plane's "black box" was never found (or had been removed). Eyewitnesses claimed that President Roldós, concerned about an assassination attempt, had traveled in two airplanes. At the last moment, it was reported, one of his security officers had convinced him to board the decoy airplane. It cost him his life.

Meanwhile in Panama, head of state Omar Torrijos (known as "Jefe de Gobierno" [Chief of Government]) eulogized President Roldós and referred to him as "my brother Jaime." He told his family, "I'll probably be next. Reagan wants me dead."

Torrijos was a hero to people in many countries; he was lauded as the man who in 1977 negotiated the Torrijos-Carter Treaty that forced the United States to relinquish the Panama Canal to Panama. Like President Roldós, he was a champion of human rights, a head of state who had opened his arms to refugees across the political spectrum. He was a charismatic voice for social justice, not just in Panama but for all of Latin America and the world. He was the David of a small country who had stood up to the Goliath of the world's strongest superpower. He had become an international figure who, many believed, would be nominated for the Nobel Peace Prize.

All those heroic qualities also made Torrijos a target. Very powerful men hated him. President Reagan, Vice President Bush, Secretary of Defense Weinberger, and the Joint Chiefs of Staff were determined to get rid of him. The heads of the US military forces in Latin America were furious about provisions in the Torrijos-Carter Treaty that closed the School of the Americas and the US Southern Command's tropical warfare center—both located in Panama and considered to be strategic to US foreign policy and hated by Panamanians and many other Latin Americans. Among Torrijos's powerful corporate enemies were the executives of the huge multinationals that had close ties to US politicians and were involved in exploiting Latin American labor forces and natural resources. They included manufacturing and engineering corporations, communications companies, and shipping and transportation conglomerates whose executives saw Torrijos as not just the leader of Panama but also as a voice for change that was being heard across the globe.

I'd been sent to Panama to corrupt Torrijos several times before the crucial negotiations in 1977 between him and President Jimmy Carter over control of the Panama Canal. My job was to convince Torrijos that he and his family and friends could become wealthy if he would only capitulate. All he had to do was allow the canal to continue as a US government corporation, keep the Canal Zone as a US territory—a swath of land with golf courses and colossal colonial-style buildings that bisected the entire country and was an affront to Panama's sovereignty—and stop campaigning for human rights and against US interventionism.

However, once I got to know this president, I was torn. My personal times with him and at events where I observed him mingling with people from all walks of life made a profound impression on me. I admired him for his courage, his sense of humor in the face of adversity, his love of life, and his political integrity. My job of trying to corrupt a man whom I respected made me question my own integrity. On the one hand, I wanted to convince him to change his policy—that was my assignment. On the other hand, his dedication to his people and a more just world made me secretly hope that he would succeed. I also realized that if I failed, he would become a prime target for the jackals. During my last meeting with him, I realized that he would not give in to me or any threats or bribes.

Two months after Roldós's death, on July 31, 1981, Torrijos was killed—along with four aides and two pilots—in a private plane crash that was strikingly similar to that of Ecuador's president. Once again, government heads and media around the world accused the US of assassinating him. I had every reason to believe they were right. The suspicions increased when it was discovered that classified documents about the investigations around the crash were destroyed by US forces when the United States invaded Panama in December 1989.

In one of those twisted ironies of life, that same July I was living with, and would soon marry, Winifred Grant, the daughter of the chief architect of Bechtel, an engineering company that had been heavily involved in Panama. It was another instance of my double life. Once again, I was pulled in two directions.

7

THREATENED

ALTHOUGH RELIEVED THAT I'D QUIT the EHM business, I was personally devastated by the deaths of these two presidents who were my clients and by the implications surrounding the high probability that my country had ordered their assassinations. I felt personally responsible. Haunted by guilt and obsessed with a desire to vindicate myself, I spent many hours in the Boston Public Library digging deep into the history of US involvement in our hemisphere.

I learned things never taught in business school. The 1823 Monroe Doctrine and the idea of Manifest Destiny, popular with many Americans during the 1840s, asserted that the United States had the right to invade any nation in the Caribbean and Central and South America that refused to back US policies. US presidents, from Teddy Roosevelt to Ronald Reagan, cited these two doctrines as justification to expand Washington's Pan-American activities. Furthermore, stories ranging from the slaughter of Native Americans to the atrocities of the Vietnam War included references to *American colonialism.*

The more I read, the more I understood that we in the United States are fed false perceptions about our history. We want to believe that we are advocates of justice and protectors of democracy, when in fact, as my job as an EHM symbolized, our story has included a great deal of colonization. People like me have promoted policies that were totally antidemocratic and destructive to cultures and economies since the beginning of our nation. I had to admit that I might have been duped at first, but I'd convinced myself to stay in even after I realized that what I was doing was wrong. I'd bought into the false perception. When these dark thoughts overwhelmed me, I tried to shake them off by recalling Entsá's advice that when we change perceptions we alter reality.

Something else also brought me down: the fact that, after a decade of making money at MAIN, I was out of work. I was thirty-six years old, without a job. Looking back, I think that, although I loved her deeply, my feelings of being a failure were instrumental in driving me to ask Winifred to marry me at that time. She had a job and she assured me that I'd soon find something. Our daughter, Jessica, was born in May 1982.

I was ecstatic to have this beautiful, amazing child in my life. At the same time, I asked myself: How can I support a family and not sell my soul?

The answer came through a new national awareness about the need for non-polluting, renewable forms of energy—and a Congress that passed a law, known as PURPA, supporting the emerging technologies. With a couple of partners, in 1982 I founded Independent Power Systems (IPS), an alternative energy company where I would serve as CEO for the next decade. We financed and built a precedent-setting, waste-burning power plant that did not produce acid rain, which was considered the major air pollutant at that time. While I was now financially successful and was able to assuage at least some of my conscience by developing environmentally friendly projects, I felt a deep sense of remorse as the EHM model spread into parts of Africa, Asia, and the Middle East.

And, my nightmares continued. Winifred would wake me at night. "You were screaming again," she'd say. I had dreams of forests destroyed by oil rigs, rivers turned black with toxic wastes, and children dying from polluted food and water. While I confided in her about the guilt I felt over what had happened in a few of the countries where I'd worked, I did not share details about my EHM role or the jackal aspects.

By 1986, I knew I had to do something more than just develop energy projects that weren't as polluting as the old models. During high school, I'd had my heart set on becoming a writer. Now might be the right time, I thought. The exploits of an EHM seemed like good material. I would reveal the truth behind this corrupt and exploitative system.

One morning, following dinner with an editor who advised me to include the true stories of other people who had held jobs similar to mine, I decided I should write a book that would be a collection of first-person accounts. I started calling former associates.

A couple of evenings later, I received a phone call. A muffled voice threatened to kill my daughter and me. "You're smart enough to stop contacting people in the business," he said in the distorted voice of a man who knew how to sound menacing, the voice of an assassin, a jackal.

I was terrified. I couldn't sleep that night. I tossed and turned and by morning the sheets were drenched in sweat. I did not tell Winifred about the phone call, but over breakfast, she said, "John, you can't go on like this. We can't go on like this."

I took a long walk in the woods and agonized over what to do. The only thing I came up with was that I had to obey the voice and stop calling people about the book. But, beyond that? Should I return to the economic consulting business? Could I find a job that wouldn't compromise my conscience? Could I write the book in a different way?

That evening I received a phone call from a former MAIN vice president, an old friend. He informed me that he wanted to set up a lunch meeting for me with the president of the company he now worked for. It was one of the world's largest and most powerful engineering corporations at that time, Stone and Webster Engineering Company (SWEC). It seemed that my problems might be solved when he told me, "SWEC needs a guy like you to work for them."

While the SWEC president and I sat together in a posh restaurant, he spoke glowingly about my rise through the ranks at MAIN and as CEO of IPS. He said he'd like to use my résumé in some of SWEC's proposals and that he was prepared to pay me a consultant's retainer of half a million dollars. I might be called on to take an occasional trip to support the company, but I wouldn't have to do much else. He lifted his martini. "To you," he said. "To us."

Our glasses clinked. A wave of relief swept through me. I couldn't believe my good fortune. Half a million dollars! I'd been liberated. Offered what was an unbelievable amount of money—for doing next to nothing. It seemed too good to be true.

And it was.

He sipped his martini, then set his glass down. "I've heard you're writing a book about our profession." His eyes met mine. "You can't do that."

The walls of the restaurant spun around me. I thought about the jackal's threats, my infant daughter. I put my hands on the table to ground myself and then, seeing how closely he watched me, reached for my martini and tried to look nonchalant as I took a drink. The familiar taste steadied me. I knew what I had to do. I set the glass back on the table. "I'd considered writing a book like that but I decided against it."

"So, you won't write it?"

I nodded.

"Is that a promise? Nothing about our type of business."

"Yes."

His eyes dropped to his martini. "Good." He raised his glass. I followed. They clinked again. "A wise man."

After that, he said it was OK for me to write about the Indigenous cultures he'd heard I loved. "In fact," he added, "it might help our business."

I barely heard him. My conscience was screaming at me: carrot and stick. The weapons I'd employed as an EHM had turned on me. I'd been hit. First, the threat; then, the reward. I'd just given in and locked myself in a cage of guilt and silence. Corporate colonialism had enslaved me.

I became chronically depressed. In an attempt to overcome it, I resumed a strenuous martial arts training, delved deep into meditation, and perfected the practices I'd been secretly learning from shamans as I traveled around the world. The latter included a visualization technique that helped me relax and focus on releasing at least some of my negative feelings. Attitudes toward shamanism and other New Age approaches had changed drastically during the 1980s. I now felt comfortable talking and writing about those aspects of my life and about my experiences as a Peace Corps volunteer.

I wrote my first book, *The Stress-Free Habit*, in 1986. Although it was not published until a couple of years later, I immediately began to write a second, *Psychonavigation*. I was careful to avoid any reference to my EHM work. These books described teachings from the Amazon, but I made no attempt to return there.

One morning in the summer of 1986 I strolled along the beach near where Winifred, Jessica, and I lived in Florida. As I looked up into the fronds of a tall palm, I felt that now familiar jab of guilt. But this time it was different; I was struck by what I needed to do as a step toward redeeming myself. I had to revisit the place that had so strongly impacted my life and which was threatened with destruction. I'd read and seen on TV that the Amazon area where I'd lived was one of the most diverse and important ecosystems on the planet and it was under attack—primarily by US oil and mining companies. Those rivers and forests were vital to our existence and, it seemed, they were also a symbol of our need to change perceptions about economic development. I knew that I needed to try to do something to reverse the damage—or at least slow it down. I realized that it was time to use those invisible darts Entsá had given me to help the forests he loved.

My contract with SWEC forced me to remain silent about EHM activities around the world—and the role they played in destroying the rain forests—but I could commit to helping the people who had kept me out of the Vietnam War and saved my life when I was dying. I wasn't sure about what I could do, but I thought that perhaps somehow I'd get to fulfill Entsá's expectations of me as a shaman.

In the two decades since my Peace Corps days, I'd been back to Ecuador as an EHM but only to the major cities on the coast and in the mountains. I had no idea how to reconnect with the Shuar deep in the jungle.

I decided to look up a businessman I'd met in Ecuador who had emigrated from France during World War II, married an Ecuadorian woman, helped the Shuar, and befriended many of us Peace Corps volunteers. That decision would change my life in ways I never anticipated.

PART 3

CHANGING THE DREAM

1987–1993

The world is as you dream it.
Your people dreamed of huge factories,
tall buildings, as many cars as there are
raindrops in this river. Now you begin to
see that your dream is a nightmare.

8

REDEMPTION

HENRI KOUPERMANN OWNED the Hotel Cuenca during my Peace Corps days. His restaurant offered the only gourmet French cooking in town. Henri gifted us volunteers with generous discounts on our birthdays and other special occasions. He had a deep respect for Indigenous people, something that was unusual among Ecuador's business community in the late 1960s. And, once when I was taken with a high fever, he nursed me back to health with nutritious food and liberal doses of French Cognac.

Arriving at Henri's hotel in 1987, I was directed to an office across the street—a travel agency—where I was greeted by a tall, muscular man with long black hair and a short black beard. He might have been mistaken for a Hell's Angel, except for the kindness in his smile, the twinkle in his brown eyes, and the softness in his voice. He shook my hand. "How can I help you?"

"I'm looking for Mr. Koupermann."

He laughed. "I am Mr. Koupermann. I suppose you wanted my father, though."

"You're Henri's son?"

"Yes. I'm Daniel. My dad passed away some years ago." He nodded toward a chair. "Can I be of service?"

We sat in his office and drank coffee, as I described my Peace Corps experiences.

"Colonization," he said. "So, you were part of that program?"

"I'm afraid so."

"A terrible idea."

I described my efforts to expose the problems by writing letters to Peace Corps and USAID officials.

"Good for you. But . . ." He frowned. "The place where you lived back then, what you call El Milagro, isn't in the jungle now. The roads arrived. The trees cut down."

It seemed impossible. "But it was deep in the forest."

"That colonization program started the destruction. Modern bulldozers finished it. They changed everything." He sighed. "For years this country pushed for economic development. I'm afraid that has resulted in an economy that is killing our most valuable resource, the environment. It's not at all the perception that was fed to us."

"How terribly sad." I did not want to admit that I was one of the people who had promoted that perception.

"Yes." He was silent for a moment. "Very sad." He leaned toward me. "You really don't want to go to your old community."

I told him about my training with Entsá and then about my EHM activities. I explained that I wanted to help the Shuar protect their rain forests, even going so far as to mention that I was driven by guilt over my role as an EHM.

"Redemption." He gave me that gentle smile that I would later come to see as a true reflection of his character. "I don't know Entsá, but I can get you to another shaman who lives with just the people you need to meet."

The next morning, flying over a sea of green, I peered down at the vast canopy of jungle that stretched for nearly three thousand miles, all the way from the Andes to the Atlantic Ocean, an area larger than the continental United States, and I was overwhelmed with nostalgia. I'd returned to a familiar place that was lodged deep in my heart. I closed my eyes.

Horrible images came to me: dams I had helped finance, industrial parks, the shah of Iran's palace, Ecuador's President Jaime Roldós standing before a huge crowd giving the last speech of his life, and mammoth derricks spilling oil into a ravaged rain forest.

When I opened my eyes, I was dazed. I peered through the window, down at a river that snaked through the trees. On the bank was a tiny clearing with several thatched-roof oval homes. It could have been Entsá's community. The single-engine plane descended and landed on a muddy airstrip.

I spent the next week in the jungle with the Shuar. I discovered that this was not at all like either the El Milagro I'd known or Entsá's community. During the two decades since my Peace Corps days, Shuar life had changed. The roads had penetrated much deeper into the jungle, their territory had shrunk, and they could no longer live as hunter-gatherers. They had taken to clearing small patches of forest and raising cattle. Unlike the Peace Corps and colonists, they understood that if the cleared areas were small enough, the roots from surrounding trees would hold the soil in place. Most of the men under thirty spoke Spanish as a second language. Many had left the rain forest and gone to work in the cities or for the oil companies.

The shaman I met, Numi, was about eighty years old. Although tiny like Entsá and stooped with age, he was amazingly energized. His fiery hypnotic eyes conveyed a sense of timeless knowledge.

When I told him about my training with Entsá, he informed me that he'd known my teacher, who'd lived his last years a day's walk away. Then he gave me a knowing smile. "His spirit calls you." As we sat together on a knoll overlooking the river, he spoke words I needed to hear.

"The world is as you dream it. Your people dreamed of huge factories, tall buildings, as many cars as there are raindrops in this river. Now you begin to see that your dream is a nightmare." He picked up a small stone. "The problem is your country is like this pebble." He threw it into the river. "Everything you do ripples across the mother." He smiled. "All you have to do is change the dream of your people."

I asked about the role of the Shuar in all this.

"We're not the problem," he replied. "Don't try to change us. Your way of life is the problem, your dream of materialism, your determination to impose your destructive ways on us. However, if some of your people want to understand about changing the dream, you can bring them here to learn." He held up a hand. "Entsá saw this coming." He gave me a solemn look. "But be careful. The oil companies will try to destroy you. Your government, as well as Ecuador's, may come after you."

9

DREAM CHANGE

I THOUGHT ABOUT NUMI and his community as I flew home. Although saddened by the changes I'd seen, I was also excited by the prospect of actually doing something, of bringing people into the jungle to learn from the Shuar to change the dream, a perception that was threatening to destroy life as we know it. I now saw it as imperative that we alter our mind-sets, our business models, and our way of life, and we needed to help decolonize the peoples whom we had colonized—as well as ourselves. But there was that other voice, a warning inside me that echoed Numi's words: The oil companies will try to destroy you. And, as if I needed the reminder: Beware the jackals who threatened Jessica and you.

I mulled it over for several days. I talked with other authors and activists I'd met. Winifred encouraged me. "You won't be happy unless you follow your heart," she said.

In the end, I knew I had to take people to Numi's community. The only question: How could I organize it in a manner that would protect my family and me? I decided that my best insurance would be to create a nonprofit. A lawyer friend helped me incorporate Dream Change as a 501(c)(3) nonprofit in 1987.

During the next couple of years, other people joined me. We wrote books, taught workshops, and partnered with Daniel Koupermann to lead trips to both Shuar and Quechua shamans so that participants could learn directly from them about the power of changing reality by altering our perceptions. I often spoke out at universities and other venues against the devastation caused in Ecuador by the oil companies—and by the modern, industrialized world's obsession with materialism and the US's determination to create a global empire.

In 1991, Daniel told me that he wanted to work with the Shuar's neighbors, the Achuar. I had not met them but had heard scary rumors about them during my Peace Corps days. I remembered a morning in 1969 spent talking with Captain Espinoza, an Ecuadorian army officer who led a ranger unit that protected Texaco's seismology teams from Indigenous warriors. He and I were sitting on a wooden bench in Sucua, a frontier town on the edge of the forest that reminded me of movies about the American Wild West. Its streets were mud, people lived in ramshackle wooden huts, and its saloons had outdoor privies. Horses were tied to hitching rails, and nearly every man carried a muzzle-loaded single-shot rifle. We were waiting for the one thing that connected Sucua to the outside world, a World War II vintage DC-3. Since it couldn't reach high enough altitudes to fly over the Andes and had no radar, its pilot had to navigate through cloud-enshrouded canyons cut by glacier-fed rivers relying only on a stopwatch and a compass: bank ten degrees to the right after two minutes, five degrees to the left after another ninety-two seconds . . .

"The Achuar are killers, butchers," Captain Espinoza had said. He ran his finger across his throat. "They're savages who'll hack off your head. Stay away from them."

My Shuar friends confirmed this. "Our worst enemies," they told me. "Don't go near them."

I related my memories to Daniel. He laughed. "That was twenty years ago. Things are different now. Their way of looking at the world has changed." He told me that he wanted to find activities the Achuar could do to maintain themselves, without depending on oil. He'd landed on ecotourism. "It's not a long-term solution," he admitted. "But it can help them begin to learn to cope with the modern world that every year is becoming more a part of their lives." He had discussed this with the Achuar. "They are very democratic," he said. "Every impacted community must agree. I spent many long nights in different communities, and in the end, they reached a consensus that they had to change the way they relate to the outside world. They asked me to help them build an ecolodge and to bring in people who want to experience and learn from them and the rain forest."

What he was telling me was a vivid example of how people alter the reality of their lives by changing their perceptions.

Drawing on his father's experience and reputation as a hotelier, Daniel obtained financing from a wealthy Ecuadorian to build an ecolodge in Achuar Territory. He moved into a pristine and wild part of the rain forest to oversee the building of a facility that would honor nature while at the same time offering comfortable accommodations to people accustomed to modern life. It would be built by the Achuar themselves, in the style of their homes, using only materials from the forests—no plastic or metal, not even nails. Nothing would be imported except for modern plumbing. It would consist of a communal dining room, a meeting lodge, and eighteen cabins with modern bathrooms. All of it would be constructed at a place the Achuar called Kapawi. It was more than a hundred miles from the nearest road through dense unexplored jungle and was next to a lake fed by the Capahuari River, one of the headwaters of the Amazon. Daniel's vision was that guests would take walks through the rain forest with Achuar guides, as well as having the opportunity to drift down the Capahuari and see the endangered freshwater pink dolphins. Part of the financing deal guaranteed that the Achuar would be trained to operate and manage the lodge; its ownership would be completely turned over to them. Daniel ended up spending three years living in the jungle and adapting to Achuar ways to help oversee the construction.

Neither Daniel nor I guessed at that time that his commitment to the Achuar would lead to changes that would stretch around the planet. However, it took a Quechua woman from the Andes to teach me how to see more clearly the relationship between perceived and objective reality.

10

TWO REALITIES

FROM 1991 TO 1993, WHILE Daniel was involved with the Achuar and I was still officially a consultant to SWEC, I continued to lead groups for Dream Change to Amazonian and Andean shamans. SWEC asked very little of me and the objective of the Dream Change trips was to teach people from the modern world about the traditions and philosophies of the Indigenous cultures.

One of the shamans I met at the time was a Quechua woman. Although she was a member of the same linguistic group as the brickmakers of my Peace Corps days, she lived near Otavalo, a couple hundred miles north of Sinincay. Her family name came from her native language, Yamberla, but she had Spanish first and middle names that amused Americans: Maria Juana. It sounded like the plant that at that time was both popular and illegal in the United States.

Although I had learned that the Quechua brickmakers' shaman, Maria Quischpe, had died, Maria Juana reminded me of her. She too wore long navy-blue skirts and embroidered blouses. Her brown eyes spar-kled, despite the age lines around them, and her smile radiated love and vitality. She had an energy about her that struck me as similar to Maria Quischpe's. She lived in a small adobe hut in an Andean valley—at over eight thousand feet in altitude—that lay at the center of a triangle formed by three volcanoes revered by her people as powerful spirits: Imbabura (male), Cotocachi (female), and Mojanda (androgynous). She told me that her parents had been shamans and had known that she was destined to follow in their footsteps when they heard her sing from her mother's womb. Now at around sixty years old, she was extremely knowledgeable and particularly eloquent at expressing the philosophy behind the idea of dream changing.

"There are two realities," Maria Juana told one of our groups, as I translated. "Objective, like this chair, and perceived, the ideas discussed while sitting in this chair. By changing perceived reality, we transform objective reality." She touched the chair. "If I told you that only a shaman is allowed to sit in this chair, it would have a different reality for you than if I offered it to you to sit in. Religion, culture, even countries are created from thoughts, ideas. After enough people accept these ideas, they become reality." She smiled. "Change the dream."

Her words echoed the teachings of Entsá and Maria Quischpe and the experience of the brickmakers. However, the straightforward and simple way Maria Juana expressed it made it easy to understand the impact perception has had on human reality over the centuries.

When people asked her for advice on how to change the dream, she responded, "It's simple; just change the story we tell ourselves. That alters the way we think about ourselves."

Returning to the United States, I began to speak about this at New Age and college conferences and workshops and to meet with others who were exploring the subject. There was a surge of interest in shamanism and ideas around what many referred to as "alternative realities" during the early to mid-1990s that coincided with the publication of my books on Indigenous cultures and shamanism—the ones that were not prohibited by my SWEC contract—my lectures, and the work we were doing through Dream Change.

I learned that there are many examples of how human history is completely molded by humans. Reality, as we know it from the standpoint of human institutions, is the result of our perceptions. The following are two of those examples that I especially liked to cite in my lectures and workshops.

Before Copernicus published his revolutionary work in 1543, people perceived the earth as the center of the universe. That belief impacted religion, science, philosophy, medicine—all the stories that shaped human reality at the time. When Copernicus proved that the earth revolved around the sun, it changed our whole way of thinking about ourselves.

In 1773, nearly everyone in the American colonies thought the British army was invincible. But George Washington had seen a British force estimated at fifteen hundred men and led by one of England's most experienced generals defeated and thoroughly routed by about nine hundred French and Indians at the Battle of the Monongahela in 1755 during the French and Indian War. "The British aren't invincible," Washington said. "We just need to hide behind trees." It changed the colonists' perception of England's power and ultimately ended British rule.

People sometimes pointed out to me that the idea that perceptions create reality is basic to modern psychotherapy and quantum physics and that it has been a driving force behind art and literature for centuries.

After a talk about shamanism I gave at a conference in California in 1992, I was approached by Bob Graham, the founder and chairman of Katalysis, a nonprofit that supported Mayan women's microcredit cooperatives in Central America. Bob invited me to join his board.

Now, here it was, only a few months later. Bob had asked me to escort Lynne Twist to Guatemala, and I found myself on this 1993 trip that was taking us deep into the Mayan Mountains. Lynne's job was to find venues where Katalysis's board members and major donors could meet with the Mayan women who were the recipients of the nonprofit's funds; my job was to contact at least one Mayan shaman and invite him or her to our meetings. Bob felt that Katalysis needed to have a stronger understanding of and connection with Mayan traditions and spirituality that only a shaman could provide; he hoped I could make that happen.

This trip piggybacked on another 1993 one when I took a group of Americans to Ecuador for Dream Change. Flying out of the Quito airport to meet Lynne in Guatemala, I had serious doubts about my chances for success. Guatemala's recent political history was very different from Ecuador's. A bloody civil war had raged in Guatemala since 1960; more than two hundred thousand Maya had been killed by the repressive right-wing US-supported regime. Mayan leaders, including shamans, were at the top of the "kill" lists. They had every reason *not* to meet with Americans.

A few months earlier, I'd also traveled to Guatemala—as Lynne somehow knew. That time, it had been to negotiate a deal with a company owned by members of the right-wing regime to develop a geothermal project. It was one of those few trips SWEC had asked me to take. I'd been wined and dined and chauffeured around in bulletproof SUVs by people the Maya hated.[1] Although I could tell myself that I no longer was an EHM, I knew only too well that I still was supporting that system. In addition to the initial retainer, SWEC was continuing to pay me a hefty consultant's fee. At the same time, I was trying to help the Mayan people defend themselves against that system. As I'd told Lynne, I was indeed a man torn between two worlds.

By the time my plane touched down in Guatemala City, I wished that I'd never agreed to this trip. The man caught between two worlds was about to set foot in one where he'd made lots of potential enemies. I'd played both sides. For SWEC, I was negotiating a deal with the wealthy ruling families who were waging a war against the Mayan people. For Katalysis, I was trying to establish a bond with those same Mayan people.

PART 4

UNITING THE EAGLE AND THE CONDOR

1993

The prophecy says that five hundred years later, at the beginning of the Fifth Pachacuti—now—the opportunity arises for the Eagle and the Condor to fly together, to mate, and to produce a new offspring, higher consciousness.

11

DARK CLOUDS

I GLANCED THROUGH THE WINDOW of our Land Rover at the black wall of clouds that hovered over the surrounding Guatemalan mountains—a black wall suddenly split by a flash of lightning that was followed by the rumble of thunder. I wondered if it had been a mistake to tell Lynne so much of my story.

It was our fourth day in Guatemala. Lynne had succeeded at her job. It had been relatively easy for her to convince the Mayan women Katalysis supported to show the upcoming group some of the projects we'd financed—raising chickens, weaving textiles, and producing baskets, pottery, and other items to sell in local markets or to the tourist shops of Guatemala City. She'd reserved rooms and meeting spaces in hotels and restaurants that were close to these women's communities and that also met the needs of privileged Americans accustomed to hot showers, comfortable beds, and western food.

My job had not gone so well. I'd sent word to the Mayan leaders that I wanted to meet one of their shamans. I'd let them know about my own training and interest in shamanism. However, for two days there'd been no response from any shamans. Then, on the evening of the third day, a breakthrough. A shaman who lived high up in the mountains had sent word that he would receive us in his home in the Mayan Mountains.

Now, we were on our way into those mountains. Outside the window, coal-black phantoms crept from the black wall of clouds down the slopes. We were headed into the home of the people who were the reason bulletproof vehicles protected the rich and powerful—and me a few months earlier. This approaching storm seemed a warning of impending danger.

Images came to mind of that curve in the road where our SUV had slowed and Jorge had pointed at the place where eight Mayan men were dragged off a bus by government soldiers, lined up at roadside, and shot in front of their wives and children. Sweat soaked my armpits. I was taking Lynne into a war zone and I was a person who might be perceived as an enemy of the people we were visiting.

I shared my fears with her.

"Working for the Hunger Project in Africa, I've been through quite a lot," she said with a gentle smile. "It's easy to get paranoid. Let's not."

I nodded and peered through my window. Another flash of lightning and a deafening clap of thunder sent a shiver down my spine. I stared for a while, trying to concentrate on the dark shadows engulfing the mountains, and then made myself look away, at the backs of the heads of the two Mayan men in the front seat. I told myself that she was right, I was unreasonably suspicious; Mayan leaders would not be foolish enough to kidnap, or murder, a couple of Americans on a philanthropic mission. That idea calmed me, and then I thought about all the times I'd fallen back on the privileges I enjoy because I am a middle-class white male from the United States.

"What do you know," Lynne's voice interrupted my thoughts, "about this shaman we're about to meet?"

A gust of wind kicked dirt up in the road ahead and rattled our windows. I turned to her. "Nothing at all. I studied with Mayan Tatas and Nanas—their titles for male and female shamans—in Mexico's Yucatán Peninsula. That's all." I let out a long breath. "That was back in the '70s when I took a leave of absence from MAIN. But I've no idea what to expect here."

"Those Mexican shamans—what did they teach you?"

"They talked a lot about lessons learned from the ancient Maya." Her question offered a welcome opportunity to focus on something other than the oppressive mountains, the menacing storm, and the anxiety I felt. I explained that the Mayan cities—including the massive pyramids and temples—were built on cement-like platforms erected in the swamps. Millions of trees were cut and the swamps drained. "It appears," I continued, "that only the royal families, nobles, and priests—the rulers—resided full time in the cities. Everyone else probably lived outside of the cities most of the time and were required to provide goods and services such as labor, jewelry, art, clothes, and food for the rulers. In exchange, the priests performed ceremonies and rituals that, they claimed, brought abundant crops and prosperity to all the people. Over time, as more and more forests were cut and swamps drained, the climate changed. There was less rain. The aquifers dried up. Crops failed. Cities went to war against other cities. Losing faith in their rulers, the people retreated into the forests and up into the mountains. The jungle took over. For hundreds of years, most of the world had no idea that towering pyramids and the ruins of a vast civilization lay hidden beneath the tree-covered mounds that dotted Central America."

"Seems like a message," Lynne said, "for what we're doing to our planet today."

Lightning lit up the sky; this time the thunder was so close that it seemed to shake our Land Rover. In the eerie light, scrawny bushes beside the road were doubled over by the wind. The dark clouds, like a sorcerer's black cape, had obliterated the mountains.

Lynne let out a sigh. "I hope we're not driving into that."

Up ahead on my side of the road, a group of men, women, and children bundled in heavy ponchos, heads down against the wind, came toward us. Our driver slowed. As we drove past them, one of the men lifted his head and peered into my window. The Land Rover sped on. I turned to watch that man. He raised a fist, spit on it, and shook it at me.

An involuntary shudder ran through my body.

Lynne was looking the other way, out her window, oblivious to what had happened.

The Land Rover took us higher, ever closer to the wall of clouds. Lynne began to talk about her experiences in Africa and India. She described her commitment to ending global starvation, and the progress she was making at raising millions of dollars for the Hunger Project. Her words, her voice, her passion to help humanity made me almost forget about our circumstances. And then it occurred to me that being on the giving, rather than the receiving, end of philanthropy was one more privilege that both she and I enjoyed.

Then, the Land Rover stopped.

I looked out at a bleak and forlorn landscape. And a small adobe hut.

Jorge turned to face us. "We're here."

12

THE STONES

"A STROKE OF LUCK." Jorge opened Lynne's car door. "The storm passed to the east."

I got out and saw that the blackest clouds had moved around us, into the distance. A cold, dank wind blew down from the nearby peaks.

Jorge led us toward the small adobe hut, up a dirt path that crunched beneath our feet. He knocked on the chiseled wooden door. Lynne clutched my arm. "Perhaps he's not here." She sounded hopeful.

Jorge knocked again.

The door creaked open. A man in a red-and-black checkered shirt stood before us. Jorge spoke to him in Mayan. The man looked us up and down and nodded grimly at Jorge but did not utter a word. The door closed.

We waited. No one spoke. The cold wind moaned. Lynne pulled her coat around her.

I had a bad feeling. As I'd told Lynne, I had no information at all about this shaman. He might hate Americans for the damage we'd done to his culture and land and have lured us in to do something to publicly humiliate us—or worse. "I think we should leave," I said.

Just then the door opened again. The man in the checkered shirt stood there. He stepped aside, revealing another man in the shadows. Arms folded across his chest, this second man wore blue jeans and a dark blue shirt. A red bandana covered his head. He spoke rapidly in Mayan to Jorge, then turned his back on us.

Jorge entered and motioned for us to follow.

I stepped into the dark room, lit only by a small window in the back wall and the open doorway. The smell of copal, an incense used in Mayan ceremonies, was almost overwhelming. A couch and two wooden chairs hugged a low wooden table. Mayan tapestries hung from the walls. The man in the checkered shirt closed the door, reducing the light to just a hazy glimmer from the tiny window. He stood, shadow-like, his back to the door, watching us.

"This is Tata Roberto Poz," Jorge said, looking at the man in the bandana who was lowering himself into one of the wooden chairs.

I held out my hand.

Roberto stared at it.

I lowered my hand.

"Please have a seat." Jorge pointed at the couch.

Lynne glanced at me. I nodded, hoping to convey a confidence I didn't feel, and waved a hand toward the couch. We both sat down.

I took a deep breath and, sitting on the edge of the couch, turned to Jorge. As he translated my Spanish to Mayan, I described the work Katalysis was doing with Mayan women and explained our desire to include Roberto in our meetings so we could better understand the shamanic traditions of his people.

In the dim light, I couldn't see Roberto's face, but his fingers drummed impatiently against the arms of his chair. When Jorge finished interpreting, Roberto looked away, toward a closed door on his right. I followed his gaze, wondering who, or what, might be lurking behind that door.

Roberto turned back and stared at me. Although he spoke in Mayan and I could not understand his words, his voice vibrated with anger.

"You dare," Jorge interpreted, "ask for my help! Your government, your CIA, and your army supported the invasion of our communities all my life. You trained Guatemalan soldiers to torture and kill us. You overthrew President Arbenz, the one politician who defended us. Like the Spanish before you, you set about to rob my people of their dignity, their pride, and their lands."

I pushed myself back into the couch. I wondered about his use of *you*. Jorge was translating it in Spanish as the familiar and personal *tu*, rather than the more general and formal *usted*. Was that significant? Was there a difference in Mayan? I had no idea, but I feared that he knew about my specific role as an EHM and was accusing me personally of being the one who had done these things, rather than applying it to Americans in general.

Roberto leaned forward. His face, dark in the shadows, came so close to mine I could smell his warm breath. "Now you ask for my cooperation," he hissed. "Do you think I'm crazy?"

"We came here," I said, attempting to maintain a steady voice, "out of respect, because we were told you're a wise person and a leader among your people." I paused, giving Jorge a chance to interpret and me time to choose my words. "I totally agree with all you just said. I too am angry at the US government and the role it's played in your civil war—and in colonizing you." I waited. When there was no response, I went on. "The only reason I can think of for why you might want to help us is so that together your people and mine can build bridges." Again, I paused. Again, no response. "Many of us in the United States hate the ways our government and a few corporations treat your people. We want to change that. We need you to help us see new ways, to help us move beyond the actions that have hurt your lives and the lives of so many others around the world, including our own."

"Words!" His fist struck the arm of his chair. "We've heard those lies before."

My eyes met his. "The lies came from others, not me." The irony of those words hit me as I spoke them. What I said was true, yet I also was that man caught between two worlds; I still worked for one of those corporations and I had often lied while doing my EHM work.

He glared at me, his eyes burning into mine.

"You can check about Katalysis," I continued. "We've done a lot to help your people, especially your women, with microcredit."

He uttered a sour laugh. "A trick. We know your tricks." He waved his hand, a dismissal. "No more."

I glanced at Lynne. She was staring down at the table. I could think of nothing more to say.

Roberto rose from his chair.

The voice of Maria Juana came to me. She had said that to change perceptions and, through them, reality, "just change the story we tell ourselves."

That morning, as I'd left the hotel, I'd spied the woven bag I'd brought from my trip to Ecuador—a gift from a Quechua shaman who lived near Maria Juana. On impulse, I'd picked it up and carried it with me. Now, it lay on the floor, next to my foot. In it were an ancient stone ax head, a carved Incan cross, and other items the shaman had given me that were sacred to his people. I picked up the bag, laid it on the table between us, opened it, and removed the stones.

Roberto had started to walk away, but now he turned, glanced down at the table, and gasped. He bent over and carefully examined the objects. His eyes met mine. "Where did you get these?" he asked in Spanish.

I explained that they had been given to me by a Quechua shaman in Ecuador named Don Esteban Tomayo. Jorge did not bother to translate.

Roberto sat down in his chair. He sucked in a long breath and released it slowly. For several long moments, he stared at the objects on the table in front of him. Then he leaned forward, held his fingers above the ax head and moved his hand in a circular motion over all the objects. He raised his head to me. "I know Don Esteban."

I was amazed. "You know him?"

"We never met in person. But yes, through shamanic journeys." His Spanish was impeccable.

"His son is my godson," I said.

He stared at me. "You're Don Esteban's compadre?"

I nodded.

He lowered his hand closer to the items laid out before him. "May I?"

"Of course."

He picked up the ax head and the Incan cross, examined them carefully, and replaced them on top of the bag. He repeated this with each of the other objects and then gently lifted the bag and the items, touched them to his heart, stood, and held my bag and the objects out toward the closed door on his right, the same door that not long before had seemed menacing. "Come with me, please. Both of you."

Lynne and I followed him. He opened the door to a small room. Filled with lit candles, it sparkled so brightly that my eyes had to adjust.

The only furniture in the room was a wooden table covered with Mayan artifacts, crystals, and other stones. It was a shaman's altar.

Roberto smiled at us and then gently pushed some of the artifacts apart, creating a space in the center. He laid my bag with its contents in that space. He brought a ceramic bowl to the front and, with one of the candles, lit something in the middle of the bowl. Smoke and the smell of copal. He spoke Mayan words, an invocation, while slowly waving the bowl of burning copal over the objects on the table.

13

THE CEREMONY

THREE MONTHS LATER, IN 1993, Lynne and I were seated in chairs on a slightly raised platform in a meeting room of a hotel in Totonicapan, Guatemala, before a group of Katalysis's board members and financial supporters.

Roberto Poz sat ramrod straight in the chair between us. His face expressionless, he was dressed in the traditional clothes of a Mayan shaman: white blouse and white slacks, a wide red sash wrapped around his waist, and a red cloth with embroidered Mayan symbols covering his head. The room held the smell of the copal he had burned to purify it. The sacred items I'd brought from Ecuador on that previous trip lay on a table before us, along with some of the pieces we'd seen on his altar that day.

I found myself thinking about the recent demise of the Soviet Union. That and this new relationship we seemed to be developing with the Maya made me wonder whether, now that the US was the world's only superpower, we would drop the old colonial, EHM tactics and instead take this opportunity to demonstrate the benefits of true democracy. Looking back, I'm surprised by my own naivete. I might have guessed that the US would squander that opportunity, that we would continue to exploit resources and create a military presence in more than a hundred countries, that we would defend brutal dictators as long as they cooperated with our policies and overthrow democratically elected presidents who did not, that we would ravage the planet's resources and devastate fragile environments, and that we would become history's largest empire.

In the weeks since our last visit, Lynne and I, along with Katalysis's founder and chairman, Bob Graham, and its executive director, Jerry Hildebrand, had talked by phone or in person with each of the people who would become members of our party. We'd made sure they understood that the trip would involve traveling through country that was torn by a civil war. We told them that we had rented our own bus and driver, would stay in the best hotels available, and had done everything possible to insure their safety. But we wanted them to know that the Maya had suffered terribly during the civil war, the US had backed ruthless dictatorships, and our country was seen by the Mayan people as supporters of a genocidal campaign against them. We warned these prospective participants that we were not at all certain about what would happen once we were in Guatemala.

Over the phone, we had heard excitement and fear. Several people declined to go because it was just too risky. They had families to consider, they told us, or jobs; we could hear the anxiety in their voices. In the end, thirty men and women, mostly white Americans, joined us.

That first night in Totonicapan, Lynne and I described the process involved in finding and convincing Roberto Poz to join us. We summarized the tragic history of the Mayan people and the role the US played in financing and supporting the military operations of repressive governments. I then gave a brief summary of the Prophecy of 2012, as it had been told to me by Viejo Itza and other Mayan shamans in Mexico's Yucatán Peninsula during the 1970s. It is one of many versions.

"According to this prophecy," I told them, "there was a long period, hundreds of years, ruled by a king who drove the world into darkness. Usually referred to as Seven Macaw, he was violent, egotistical, and obsessed with materialistic things. During his reign, the forests were cut and the swamps drained in order to build cities. The natural resources were depleted. There were huge gaps between the few very rich and the rest of the people. Severe changes in the climate resulted in massive crop failures. Then wars broke out between the cities. There was more brutality and chaos.

"The legend continues that two young siblings, known as the Hero Twins, cut off the head of Seven Macaw and threw it into a basket. They replaced Seven Macaw with a compassionate, selfless leader, Hunahpu, who inspired people to live environmentally sustainable and spiritually fulfilling lives. The year 2012 is important because the Mayan calendars that go back thousands of years will end then and Seven Macaw will be replaced by Hunahpu. The new calendars will start on December 22, 2012.

"Why that particular day?" a man asked. "Nineteen years from now."

"Long ago," I explained, "Mayan astronomers knew that, from the earth's perspective, the sun will enter the center of the Milky Way—the 'great rift,' the dark spot in the middle of our galaxy—on December 21, 2012. That moment represents the throwing of Seven Macaw's head into the basket, the beginning of the transition.

"The prophecy goes on to say that on December 22, 2012, the energy in the universe will shift. It will create the opportunity for us to look at ourselves and the world with a new mind-set about what it means to be human and adopt the values and take the actions necessary for change. That's important: for the transition to occur, we will have to act. We, men and women, the Hero Twins, must make it happen. Our leaders will not cut off their own heads; they will not initiate the important changes that are so needed, unless we force them to."

I glanced at the people in the room. "Like most legends, myths, and prophecies, this one carries an important message. It's time for each of you to ask yourself: Who and what am I? Why was I born at this particular time in human history? What actions can I take to help this prophecy become a reality? What are my fears? What is blocking me from doing it?"

A woman raised her hand. "I think," she said, "it's significant that the Twins cut off Seven Macaw's head. Leaders try to get into our heads and convince us to do what they want. I recall that the Prophecy of the Eagle and the Condor is a call for us to get out of our heads, to follow our hearts. Can you please repeat that other prophecy for us?"

I looked around the room. "OK if I continue talking?"

There were voices of "Yes" and "Please tell us."

"No one knows how old this prophecy is," I began. "Probably more than two thousand years. It may have come out of the Amazon and then traveled throughout the Andes. It says: 'Back in the mists of history, human societies took two routes. The Eagle peoples flew the path of the mind, of science, technology, and industry. The Condor peoples flew the path of the heart, of passion, intuition, and spiritual connections with nature.' It goes on to explain that for centuries they would never meet. Then in the Fourth *Pachacuti* (in Quichua, the language of the Andes, a five hundred–year interval), which began in about 1500 AD on our calendar, their paths would cross; the Eagle would nearly drive the Condor into extinction. But not quite. The prophecy says that five hundred years later, at the beginning of the Fifth Pachacuti—now—the opportunity arises for the Eagle and the Condor to fly together, to mate, and to produce a new offspring, higher consciousness.

"History confirms the first prophecy. Columbus, 1492. The Eagle swept into Condor territory and almost wiped out the Indigenous peoples. But not quite.

"Now, here we are nearly five hundred years later and the prophecy is being fulfilled again. The Eagle and Condor are coming together to create higher consciousness. It is happening! Indigenous teachers have invited us to learn their ways. There is a deep interest in traditional nature-based wisdom and shamanism among industrialized people around the world. It's happening here. The Maya, us. Right now. Today! This trip."

Once again, I looked at each of them. "Another message?" I asked and then continued, "This prophecy challenges each of us to explore what we can learn from the Condors, from Indigenous people and their traditions, ceremonies, and cultures. We all come from Indigenous ancestors. We know that Indigenous cultures have lived sustainable, earth-honoring lives for hundreds of thousands of years. Ask yourself: Why was that pattern broken? What passions and skills do I have that can help fix it? What can I do that will bring me the most satisfaction and joy and help transform a Death Economy into one that supports long-term life on this planet, a Life Economy? How do I follow my intuition?"

I stopped and looked at Lynne. She introduced Roberto.

He stood, glanced around the room, and opened his arms to embrace the entire group. He spoke a few words in Mayan. Then, his face softened and he switched to Spanish. I translated. "Welcome to my land. We are happy you have come here." He acknowledged his reluctance at first to join us. "But," he said, "now that I look out at you and feel your energy, I'm honored to be here with you."

He talked about the problems his people have endured since the Spanish conquest, the long history of colonialism by the country's wealthiest families and foreign corporations, the US's support of dictatorships, and the attempted genocide. He encouraged us to feel both the suffering and the fortitude of the Maya as we visited their communities. He especially praised the women. He told us that in addition to supporting their men, the guerrilla fighters, the women also took to the streets, demonstrated, blockaded, and often ended up wounded, jailed, or killed. He discussed the strong connection that his people have to what he referred to as "the Heart of the Earth, the Heart of the Heavens, Heart of the Water, Heart of the Fire, Heart of the Air, All Our Hearts." He emphasized that there is no separation between humans and nature. "All hearts are connected."

I was struck by Roberto's courage. He had come to confront those who represented his enemies in the hope that he could transmute the energy of hatred into compassion and cooperation.

In that moment, translating for this Mayan shaman, I also realized that I'd found my own path. I realized that on that stormy day when Lynne and I drove into the mountains, my fear had been not so much of physical violence but of facing myself and the things I'd done as an EHM.

And I understood too that all of us in that room had been forced to confront some aspect of ourselves, our cultures, or our ways of living that had been molded by antagonism, conflict, the idea that "they" are bad and "we" are good and that "our" piece of the pie must be taken from "them." As Americans, all of us had paid taxes that had helped finance an ongoing military attempt to destroy the Maya. As an EHM and consultant to SWEC, I'd played a direct role. This journey was an attempt to repair some of that damage.

In that room were two very different cultures. The Americans, the Eagles, were part of a culture that could justify an attempt to wipe out the Mayan culture for economic gain. The Condors, exemplified by Mayan leaders like Roberto Poz, prioritized people's relationships to each other, the natural world, and future generations. I wondered, If two such different cultures can treat each other with respect and teach and learn from one another, what else may be possible?

When Roberto finished speaking, he stepped down from the platform he had shared with Lynne and me and began shaking hands with the people who came to thank him. I watched as he made a point of greeting everyone personally.

Beginning the next day, we traveled by bus to the areas Lynne and I had explored, met with groups of women who were members of the microcredit programs Katalysis financed, and visited a number of their projects. We heard stories of hardship, the suffering of women widowed and children orphaned because their men had been killed or had disappeared during the civil war. And we heard them declare their determination to prevail and to ensure the continuation of their culture and traditions.

A woman named Carita told us that soldiers had come to her home in the middle of the night, dragged her husband out, tied his hands, beat him unconscious in front of her and their four children, tossed his limp body into the back of a truck, and then driven off. She never saw him again.

"He didn't do anything against the government," she said, struggling to control her emotions. "He was a farmer, not a fighter." A couple of months after his disappearance, she knew that it would be up to her alone to support her family; she joined the local Katalysis-funded microcredit cooperative and used a small loan to make the down payment on a potter's wheel and kiln. She proudly took us around her shop and showed us her work.

One of the women in our group held up a vase. "This would sell for a small fortune in a New York gallery," she said.

Carita smiled. "I don't need a small fortune. Just the $15 I'm asking. It will feed my children for a week."

By the time our group left, we had nearly emptied her shop.

Juanita Luisa had a very different story. Her husband had joined the rebels. He had lost a leg in a battle with government forces. Although he'd learned to manage on a single crutch, he could not return to his job selling produce in the local market because the soldiers who frequented that market would identify him as their enemy.

Broken, he turned to alcohol. "He's no good anymore," she confessed. "But he's my husband. I must feed him, as well as our children." She had always been a weaver; however, now, with the help of a microcredit loan, she had organized other women into a weaver's cooperative. "I'm a big business person," she laughed. "Seven amazing women. I hardly weave anymore because I spend so much time selling our things in Guatemala City."

We heard more than a dozen compelling stories as we visited these women and their projects. Katalysis people frequently expressed how much their impressions of Guatemala and its people had changed as a result of this trip. "The reality here is not at all what I'd expected," one woman said, summing up the views of many others. They admitted to being deeply moved by the ingenuity, courage, determination, and resourcefulness of these women, as well as by the women's gratitude for the role Katalysis played in their lives, and by their commitments to protecting their culture—despite attempts by ours to destroy it.

In the evenings, we assembled in hotel conference rooms to discuss the events of the day. Lynne, Bob Graham, Jerry Hildebrand, and other members of the Katalysis staff talked about the importance of microcredit. They explained that loans to women were good business, that unlike men, the women did not squander those loans on liquor, gambling, and other nonproductive activities, and that in many parts of the world microcredit had empowered women in ways they had never before experienced.

"As a result," Lynne added, "many women have become the primary breadwinners for their families. They're community leaders—and models for the next generation."

After dinner on most nights, Lynne led us through practices she had developed over the years of her work with the Hunger Project, encouraging each of us to go deeper into our feelings. Sometimes this involved two people facing each other and describing the experiences of that day that had the greatest impact on them. Sometimes people in groups of three shared what each most appreciated about the other two. Sometimes we simply exchanged stories and shared our thoughts and emotions.

Several people talked about the advantages they'd experienced all their lives because they had been born, raised, and educated in prosperous US communities. By spending time with the Maya and hearing their stories, they had gained a perspective far beyond that afforded by the media. This trip had also shown them that the privileges they took for granted often had been gained at the expense of countries like Guatemala.

On the last night, Roberto Poz invited us to join him in a traditional Mayan fire ceremony. He led us outside our hotel to an area that had been cleared of grass and brush and he instructed us to form a circle.

"Nearly every fire ceremony," he explained, "begins like this." He held up a bag of white sugar and drew a circle in the earth. "This represents oneness, the heart of the earth, the heart of the heavens, the unity of our hearts with all nature and the universe." Inside the circle he drew a cross. "The four directions and also the four elements: the sacred air, sacred water, sacred earth, and sacred fire." With the sugar, he placed a white dot in each of the four quadrants formed by the cross. "These dots represent the four times humans practically disappeared from our world." He pointed at one of the dots. "The great flood. The shamans shapeshifted us into fish. When the floods receded, we returned to humans." He pointed at another dot. "Fire. The volcanoes. We shapeshifted into birds and flew above the flames." And another. "Winds. Hurricanes. We shapeshifted into monkeys and clung to the most flexible trees." He stepped to the last dot. "The earth opened up, earthquakes. We became bats and flew into the caves." Then he drew a smaller circle in the very center, where the lines of the cross intersected. "This is now. Once again, we humans are threatened with destruction." He straightened; his eyes moved around our circle of people. "Unlike the other times, we ourselves created this disaster." He paused and looked at each of us again. "How shall we shapeshift this time?" He smiled. "We must come together, as we are doing here today, and rise to a better understanding of what it means to have the power of humans on this planet."

"Higher consciousness," someone said in Spanish.

Roberto's smile broadened. "Exactly."

He continued building the fire with small balls made of copal tree resin, colored candles, bricks of raw sugar, and little cups of chocolate that he filled with honey. We spent the next hour following Roberto's directions as he led us through a ceremony that involved reciting the days and energies of the Mayan calendar, sometimes blowing our own worries and negative thoughts and ideas into candles that we gave to the fire and, at other times, blowing the energies we needed to move forward into our own personal shapeshifts into candles and offering these to the fire.

As I watched the people from Katalysis participate in this ceremony that dates back three thousand years or more and is as old as the Mayan culture, I felt a deep sense of joy. Everyone in that circle was glowing. I couldn't help thinking that ceremonies like this and the ways those ceremonies affected their perceptions and inspired them to rise above the travails of life were the reason the Maya had survived not only all the natural catastrophes that inflicted their lands but also the onslaught of the Spanish conquistadores and the current civil war. How much better, I thought, the world would be if everyone everywhere had similar practices.

After the fire ceremony ended, some of us returned to a meeting room inside the hotel. I had described for Roberto the types of guided journeys I took people on during shamanic workshops. He asked me to demonstrate that now. I suggested that we do it together. So, aided by a drum and rattle, he and I guided the members of the group who wanted to participate into such a journey.

As people lay on mats on the floor, I asked them to envision a sacred place where they felt totally safe and secure. "It could be," I said over the sound of the drum and rattle, "a place you actually know, perhaps one you visited as a child. Or an imagined place. Explore it with whatever senses most appeal to you. If you're visual, you may see it. If not, don't worry. You may hear, smell, taste, or feel it. Or, simply think it. The word 'inspire' comes from being 'in spirit,' opening to the divine muse. Just allow whatever presents itself to happen. Don't let your head get in the way."

I whispered a translation of what I'd just said into Roberto's ear. He smiled and nodded that he agreed with that approach. "Now," I continued, "slowly begin to rise above your sacred place, as though you're flying or floating on a magic carpet. Up, higher and higher." We drummed and rattled. "Now, look down at the earth. See what you see."

We gave them about fifteen minutes to go into their own process. Roberto mostly had his eyes closed as he shook his rattle. But several times, he looked at me, grinned, and nodded his head.

After we guided the people back out of the journey, I asked them to find a partner with whom to describe their experiences. When they had finished, some of them shared with the larger group. Lynne was one of those. As she later wrote in her book, *The Soul of Money,*

> *It was my first experience with a shamanic ceremony, and as I let myself be drawn into that dream state, I had a remarkable experience . . . I became a large bird and experienced myself flying over a vast, green forest. As I looked down I saw disembodied faces floating up from the forest floor toward me. They were faces of men that were painted with geometric designs, and they wore yellow and red feather crowns. As they floated toward me, and then back into the forest, they seemed to be speaking in a strange language that I didn't know.[1]*

Lynne's journey that night turned out to be a harbinger of events that would involve her; her husband, Bill; many of their friends; the Achuar and other Indigenous people in the Amazon and Andes; and hundreds of thousands of people in more than eighty countries for decades to come. It was another step toward the jaguar we would come to understand was the one we all have to touch; this jaguar empowers us to change our ideas of what it means to be human on this planet and then do things that alter reality. The partnership we were creating, I would later realize, was part of the realization of the prophecies.

PART 5

CONFRONTING THE JAGUAR

1993

They said they had dreamed on this, that their shamans had gone deep into the meaning of their visions, and they had concluded that they have to touch us—their people have to touch our people—initiate contact with the very thing they most fear.

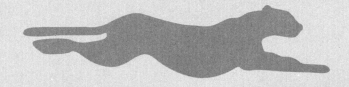

14

BLOOD LUST

"KILL! KILL! KILL!" Spears banged against my window.

Three months after the Katalysis trip to Guatemala, I was trapped inside a small plane that had just landed on a muddy airstrip deep in the Ecuadorian Amazon rain forest, near the Achuar community of Kapawi. I stared out, terrified, at the painted faces of enraged Achuar warriors. As they hammered their spears and machetes against our fuselage and windows they screamed a word I understood in their language, "Kill! Kill!"

I'd thought times had changed in the twenty-five years since that day in 1969 when Captain Espinoza warned me that the Achuar were killers. Roads had penetrated the area in Shuar Territory where I'd lived then, the fly-by-compass DC-3 had been replaced by modern radar-equipped Cessnas, and Sucua had exchanged its Wild West image for hotels that offered hot water and flush toilets.

But these Achuar still lived in their vast, remote, and roadless jungle.

"Kill! Kill!"

"Just take off," I screamed at the pilot.

"I can't," he yelled back. "They've stuck logs in front of my wheels."

"Kill Yahanua! Kill Tukupi's daughter."

Yahanua was sitting in front of me, next to the pilot. She leaned across the back of her seat. "Let them kill me." Her voice was steady. "I'm dead anyway. Your only chance is if they kill me."

Outside, the chanting grew louder. "Kill Yahanua! Kill Tukupi's daughter!"

My heart hammered at my ribs. I desperately tried to focus, to think of something to do.

Then, through the window, I caught sight of my friend Daniel Koupermann.

He'd called me several months earlier, asking me to meet with the Achuar at Kapawi.

I'd arranged to fly in and to bring three others: Juan Gabriel Carrasco, an Ecuadorian adventure travel guide; Ehud Sperling, president of Inner Traditions International, the publisher of my books on Indigenous people; and Yahanua, a Shuar woman who helped us arrange trips to her people.

The night before we landed at that airstrip near Kapawi, the four of us had visited the home of Tukupi, a Shuar shaman I'd heard stories about for many years. Yahanua was the Shuar equivalent of his goddaughter.

Tukupi lived near the border that separated Shuar from Achuar Territory. Yahanua told us that no one knew his exact age, but due to the fact he had been a war chief in some of the last great wars during the 1940s when hundreds of Shuar went up against an equal number of Achuar, they were sure that he was more than eighty years old. In later years, he had changed his ways and become a shaman.

The big wars had ended due to the efforts of Catholic missionaries, but personal animosities, based on long-standing codes of justice and revenge, continued. Since Tukupi had, by his own admission, killed more Achuar warriors than any other living Shuar—thirty-three in hand-to-hand combat—he was targeted by their sons and brothers.

Because of Tukupi's reputation as a fighter, I had envisioned a fierce, scowling old warrior, possibly shriveled with age. Perhaps it was a bias from my culture, from all the books I'd read and movies I'd seen, that I had thought of him more as a warrior than a shaman. I was wrong. My first glimpse of Tukupi was of a potbellied man wearing khaki shorts and naked above the waist. As he strolled toward us after we stepped off our plane, he reminded me of images of a smiling Chinese Buddha, except he lacked most of his teeth. While he pumped my hand, I studied the faded tattoos on his face. They reminded me of Entsá all those years ago.

"Tattoos very old," he said in halting Spanish with a laugh.

As darkness fell and the night cacophony of tree frogs took over, we sat in Tukupi's lodge. It too returned me to Eniisa and the place where I'd experienced a life-changing healing. Late into the night, Tukupi described the hand-to-hand battles he'd fought.

"Sometimes," he said in Shuar that was translated to Spanish by Yah-anua, "a warrior sent an insulting message through a young boy, like 'Your wives are ugly but I'm coming to screw them anyway. So, stay out of my way if you want to live.' Sometimes they simply said things like 'You killed my brother. You too will die.'" He laughed. "They always warned me. I used to say to them once I confronted them, before the fight, 'Why didn't you just sneak up and kill me in the night?' They would respond that the Shuar might do it that way but it was the coward's way. I'd tell them that their way was stupid; it would send them to their grave." He glanced around at us. "Then I fought and killed them with my spear or machete."

"Did you shrink their heads?" Juan Gabriel asked.

"Of course." He laughed. "I didn't want their spirits to attack me."

Sitting in that ancient warrior's home, after listening to his murmuring voice talk so simply of a warrior culture that lived on in him, I explained to Ehud the Shuar belief that when a man is killed by another, one part of his soul will return to avenge the death. By shrinking the head, that part is locked inside.

"How's it done?" Ehud asked.

At my request, Tukupi demonstrated. He ran a finger across his neck, then up the back of his head. "We cut off the head and remove everything inside—skull, brains, all of it—and give it to Tsunkui, the river goddess. We boil the skin to preserve it. After that, we sew up the eyes, ears, nose, and mouth to lock the vengeful part of the soul inside, pour hot rocks into the cavity, and mold it to be a face again. Every day, as it shrinks, we use smaller rocks. Finally, we fill it with kapok cotton and begin ceremonies that last many months to put the soul at rest."

"Put the soul to rest," Ehud said. "I like that idea. Very different from the perception we in the States have that it is a savage, gory ritual of vengeance and humiliation."

As the embers in the fire in Tukupi's lodge faded, so did the conversation. After we nestled into our sleeping bags, I had visions of shrunken heads and wondered how the Achuar felt about Tukupi these days.

Now sitting on that plane, surrounded by angry Achuar men, I had my answer.

During the more than twenty-four hours since we'd landed at Tukupi's, word had somehow reached Kapawi that we had visited their old enemy and were traveling with his goddaughter. Perhaps the news had arrived through runners or by bush radio; in any case, the warriors had been alerted.

Despite the wonderful education we'd received from Tukupi's stories, we'd made a big mistake by visiting him. These men, whose fathers and brothers had been slain by Tukupi, had a code of honor demanding that they kill Yahanua and, I imagined, the three of us who traveled with her.

"Kill! Kill Yahanua! Kill Tukupi's daughter!"

The pounding and chanting grew more intense. When I saw Daniel push his way into the seething warriors, relief swept through me. Then it occurred to me that they'd kill him too.

He made it to the plane and raised his hands. "Brothers, let me speak," he yelled in Spanish. Someone translated into Achuar. The shouting stopped. "These people are my friends." He motioned for the pilot to shut down the engine. "They come in peace."

Inside the plane, I heard the clicking of a seatbelt and the sound of the latch on the door next to Juan Gabriel. I struggled to release my own seatbelt.

The door opened and Daniel's hand reached in. "Come quickly," he said to Juan Gabriel.

I was next. The sun blinded me as I stumbled to the ground, my knees buckling, and was held up by Daniel's firm hand. I turned to watch Ehud step out.

Just then the silence was shattered by a hair-raising scream.

One of the warriors rushed toward the open doorway. He brandished a machete, shaking it violently at the plane. His face, painted with vermillion and black stripes, was contorted in anger.

Daniel quickly stepped between him and the plane. The warrior stopped inches from Daniel and glared at him. Daniel spoke to him softly and, at the same time, shut the plane's door. Yahanua and the pilot remained inside.

The Achuar men closed in around Ehud, Juan Gabriel, and me. Bodies brushed aggressively against us, shaking their weapons and resuming the chant "kill, kill, kill."

Daniel's hands went up. "Those are the old ways." His voice was controlled, calm, and steady—and so was the translator's. "The Achuar and Shuar are no longer enemies. Now, you must all join together: Achuar, Shuar, Kichwa—all the nations—to fight the oil and mining companies." He touched my shoulder. "This is John Perkins. I told you about him and his organization, Dream Change. He's here to help you."

The ground beneath my feet was spinning as Daniel ushered the three of us away from the warriors, to the shade of a nearby tree. I leaned against its trunk, trying to steady my breathing, and watched him walk back into the mob that surrounded the plane.

A face peered through the plane's window. Perhaps it was the light—or just my imagination—but for a moment I thought: Tukupi. Then I saw it was Yahanua. I waved. But she didn't seem to see me.

Daniel spoke to the milling warriors, words I couldn't quite make out. They were constantly moving, like a disturbed hive of angry bees. Several of them raised their spears high and waved them toward the plane, then all of them slowly moved away.

Daniel came to us. "I couldn't convince them." He wiped sweat from his brow. "She's got to leave."

The pilot started the engine. Slowly the plane turned around. A blast of wind from the propeller spattered us with mud. The engine revved. The plane raced down the runway, picked up speed, and rose, clearing the top of the canopy by only a few feet.

As it flew away, I glanced back at the warriors who now stood still, next to the airstrip, watching it depart. In a final gesture of hatred, they raised their spears and shouted. One turned and stared at me. His glowering expression shook me to the core.

I too was his enemy. Why hadn't I left with Yahanua? Why hadn't we all remained on that plane and flown out?

"Let's go," Daniel said. He led us down a narrow, muddy trail through thick jungle. The noise of the plane died, the birds were quiet, there was an overwhelming silence.

Five Achuar men followed; on their shoulders, the backpacks I'd forgotten we had.

"How come they're carrying our stuff?" I asked Daniel. "Shouldn't we help?"

He gave me the hint of a smile. "I've told them you're our guests. That's how they treat their guests."

It seemed to me that this was one more example of the privileges we Americans expect to receive. I supposed that at some subconscious level I'd known I didn't need to worry about the backpacks because they would be taken care of.

When we arrived at the wide Pastaza River, we stood for a moment staring at the turbulent waters that had plummeted from Andean glaciers and were headed for the Atlantic Ocean. A long dugout canoe with an outboard motor was pulled up on the river bank.

The five Achuar men loaded our packs into the canoe and sat near the stern. Daniel, Juan Gabriel, Ehud, and I climbed aboard. I glanced at the Achuar in the canoe. Not one of them met my gaze. Despite the fact that they had apparently accepted Daniel's mandate that we were their guests, they looked sullen. I suspected that they were upset that when Yahanua flew away they'd been deprived of something they considered their right. Or was I just interpreting their expressions as sullen? I hoped it was the latter.

Daniel motioned for Ehud and me to take the second seat from the front. He and Juan Gabriel sat nearest to the bow. I felt naked, exposed, vulnerable. I wished there had been some sort of barrier between my back and the Achuar. I thought of Yahanua safe in the plane, or maybe already back in her own home now.

Daniel turned to us. "Kapawi," he said, "is about two hours away." He signaled for the Achuar man in the stern to start up the outboard motor; it looked and sounded as if it might have dated back to those big wars between the Achuar and Shuar in the 1930s and '40s.

The river was raging, its swift current cluttered with logs that bobbed and bucked and threatened to ram our canoe. Whirlpools foamed around us. I knew there were caimans beneath the murky banks overhung with jungle vines. I wondered if the Achuar in our canoe wanted to spear us, throw our bodies into the river, and let the caimans eat the evidence.

My thoughts were interrupted by rain. Great sheets slanted across the river and obliterated the jungle. Daniel, Juan Gabriel, Ehud, and I huddled beneath tarps that had been stacked in the bow. We were already drenched; the tarps stank of motor oil and rotten fish, but they afforded us some protection from the pounding rain.

The deluge sounded like bullets slamming against our tarp. I'd been in jungle storms before but always beneath the treetop canopy, never this exposed, in the middle of a river. Once I lifted the tarp just enough to peer out; I saw nothing but a wall of water. I wondered how the man at the motor managed to maneuver us through the river debris.

It occurred to me that I had feared these men and yet our lives were now in their hands and they were taking care of us.

After perhaps an hour, the deluge stopped. We removed our tarps. I turned to see that the soaked Achuar men had stripped down to loincloths; they were bailing with hollowed-out gourds. I shouted back to them, asking if I could help.

"No," one of the Achuar replied. "This is our job." Again, I was struck by the difference in my earlier fear of them and the reality of the support they were giving us.

I spied a tarp near Juan Gabriel's feet that had not been used to shelter us or our luggage; it covered something bulky. I asked Daniel what lay beneath it.

He smiled, bent over, and patted it. "A present," he said.

I tried to reach between him and Juan Gabriel to uncover it.

He shoved my hand away. "It's a present," he insisted.

"For . . . ?"

His smile broadened. "Guess?"

"No idea."

He pulled off the tarp. "You."

An aluminum quarter keg of Heineken beer.

I leaned forward, between them, and touched it. It was solid, real—not a mirage. I clasped his shoulders. "You know me well!"

He just laughed.

We passed that keg around, each of the nine of us hefting it just above our mouths and drinking. At first it was heavy, but with each drink the load got lighter. As did the spirits of our group. We four sang "Row, Row, Row Your Boat." The Achuar laughed, we laughed, we drank, we sang some more; we came together in a way that helped mend the wound of Yahanua's near murder.

Our canoe turned off the Pastaza River and into a much smaller, calmer tributary. Huge trees spread their branches over us and it seemed almost as if we'd entered a protected forest tunnel.

"Feels like a cathedral," Ehud said.

Daniel turned and smiled. "The Capahuari river. Very lovely, very peaceful. One of the reasons I chose this site for the lodge."

The canoe came around a bend and suddenly the motor went silent.

"Look there," Daniel pointed, and the water ahead of us parted as two thin blades that looked like large gray knives broke the surface. "Freshwater dolphins."

"Amazing," Ehud exclaimed. "I've read about them but I never thought I'd see them."

"A good sign," Juan Gabriel said. "They're greeting us."

We sat quietly watching them as they frolicked around our canoe. Then, as quietly as they'd come, they disappeared. The motor started up and soon we arrived at the wobbly, makeshift dock at the site that would become the hotel, the Kapawi Lodge.

I felt a great sense of relief. Then Daniel said, "We meet with the community leaders tonight in their council house. They want to talk with you, John."

15

THREATS FROM TWO GOVERNMENTS

WE SAT ON HARD WOODEN BENCHES fashioned from the bottoms and sides of old dugout canoes. Achuar women constantly refilled our gourds with chicha while their warrior husbands watched to make sure we drank every drop.

One of their leaders stood before us. He held a spear in his hands. Although he spoke in Achuar, a teenage boy who had attended a missionary school translated into Spanish.

"We have heard," the speaker said, addressing me, "that you lived in Shuar Territory many years ago, before some of us were born. Back then, we knew little about the outside world. Now we are not so ignorant. The ice on the great mountains is melting. Your oil companies have poisoned the rivers of our neighbors, the Kichwa and the Huaorani. They murder women and children with their poisons and kill warriors who try to defend their lands. They drop fire from their planes. Your people have no respect for the forests and the rivers and the animals. When they come to a place, it turns to ash and black oily mud. The trees and animals vanish, never to return."

He raised his spear over his head and then lowered it. Stepping toward me, he shoved the sharp point at my face. "We are warriors." Then, to my relief, he swung the point away from me and toward the benches where the men sat. "But our shamans have had dreams that the destruction is coming our way. We are not stupid enough to think that our spears can fight your bullets, your planes, your poisons, and your fire from the sky." He showed me the end of the spear opposite the point; it had been carved into a serpent's head. "Arutam," he said, using the word common to both the Shuar and Achuar for the strength to shapeshift. He handed me the spear. "We have heard that you help the Shuar. Now, we ask the same for us. We ask you to listen to the message of this spear that represents the great spirit that is the power of the forests, Arutam. We ask you to help us touch the jaguar, the thing we fear the most, you, your people, your culture."

Many others followed him. Each speaker who stood before us, that night and the next, delivered a similar message. Some shouted, others spoke softly. Some gestured dramatically, others stood ramrod straight, hands glued to their sides. But they all had the same message, and it was one I did not want to hear.

They were asking me to form a partnership between them and people from the US who would help them fend off the oil companies, protect their forests, and—as they put it—work with them to change the dream of the modern world, to shift a culture of overconsumption to one that honors and sustains life. It was similar to the messages I'd heard before—from the Maya, the Shuar, and the Quechua. However, according to the Achuar, this was a message that came directly from the forest itself. They, and now I, were simply the messengers.

I wanted to resist—I had to resist—because I was overwhelmed already by my work with Dream Change. I felt as if I were failing the Shuar and not doing enough in my work at various venues speaking out in defense of the Indigenous people and the environment. How could I possibly take on more? How could I help these people?

And there was something else. I'd begun to have experiences that brought back Numi's warning: "The oil companies will try to destroy you. Your government, as well as Ecuador's, may come after you."

On an earlier trip to Ecuador, I'd been in my Quito hotel room when I'd received a call from an Ecuadorian man who identified himself as Julio Martinez, an advisor to the governmental organization that oversaw foreign oil contracts, Petroecuador. He invited me to dinner.

"Oil," Julio said as we sat in the posh El Dorado restaurant, "is Ecuador's future. If Dream Change and you continue to cause problems . . ." His voice trailed off. He took a sip of wine. "Well," he continued, "you knew President Roldós." He shook his head sadly. "Roldós stood in the way of progress. When his plane crashed, he paid the ultimate price." He peered over his glass at me. "Don't be so foolish."

I flew into Miami the day after that dinner meeting. As I was about to leave the US customs area, a man in a business suit flashed a badge at me and then escorted me to a private room. Without responding to my demands for an explanation, he and another man strip searched me. It was rough, humiliating, and intimidating.

I had no doubt that I was being warned—threatened by both governments.

Now, deep in the Amazon, the Achuar were urging me to take an even bigger risk. They were asking me to deliver a message from the forest to the outside world. They were asking me to form a partnership that would go head-to-head with Big Oil and change the perceptions, values, and actions of modern civilization.

16

DECISIONS

EARLY IN THE MORNING of the third day, after hearing those pleas for help from the Achuar during that first visit to Kapawi in 1993, Daniel led me along a narrow trail through dense forest. It had rained for most of the night; the air was thick with the scent of damp foliage. Water from trees, vines, and leaves dripped on my head and shoulders. Unseen birds, high in the canopy, serenaded us with songs.

Juan Gabriel and Ehud stayed back at the lodge where we had slept on the floor in sleeping bags. Ehud wanted to record a couple of the elders telling stories from their oral traditions. Juan Gabriel was translating for him.

Daniel and I arrived at a spot where the trees opened to a magnificent view of the Capahuari River, not far from the temporary dock where we had landed three days before. The sun beat down on us. Seeing the river took my thoughts back to those terrifying moments at the airstrip, the warriors who wanted to kill Yahanua. The Achuar had seemed peaceful enough since then, but I couldn't shake my feelings of anxiety. . . .

Daniel must have sensed my apprehension. "The Achuar are good people," he said. "It's tough to overcome old patterns but they're working hard at it. And they're asking you to guide your people to overcome patterns that threaten us all." He patted me on the back then pointed at the river. "This'll be the first glimpse of the Kapawi Lodge our visitors get." He spread his arms, embracing the river. "We want to make it special." He looked at me. "It's as close to paradise as you can get here on earth, don't you think?" He gave me that smile of his. "But I have to ask you, John: Do you really want to spend the rest of your life here, drinking chicha and listening to the Achuar beg you for help?"

I was stunned. "Of course not."

"Then you're going to have to agree to their request. They own the canoes."

"They wouldn't dare hold us hostage." I paused and looked into his eyes. "Would they?"

He laughed and again patted my back. "Give it some thought, John."

I spent most of the rest of the day alone, beside the river, pondering his words. I didn't think the Achuar would force the four of us, including two Americans, to stay against our wills. But, based on what I'd experienced at the airstrip, how could I be certain?

In any case, Daniel had made his point. The Achuar were persistent. They needed and wanted my help. And there was a voice inside me that told me that I wanted to help them, that perhaps it was my destiny.

I stood watching the Capahuari flow past. I thought about the American patriots who had defied the British. I thought about Robin Hood, Martin Luther King Jr., Rosa Parks. All my heroes had taken courageous stands to help the oppressed. I thought about the Petroecuador man and the US customs officials.

I closed my eyes and listened to the river and the birdsong from the forest. Entsá's face appeared. He leaned forward and, placing his mouth next to my heart, blew. His image faded. I touched my heart. I thought I could feel the darts he'd given me all those years ago. I opened my eyes.

"Of course you're afraid," I said to myself. "Isn't that the point? The oil companies and the US government are your jaguars." I spread my arms toward the river and the trees beyond. I wasn't going to run away.

I picked up a stick, held it for a moment, and threw it into the river. As I watched it float away, I knew that when I came face-to-face with my fears, I could strengthen my resolve to stand up to an imperialistic system that was contrary to the American ideals I'd been taught to embrace. I had to do that. But, how? That was the question. What could I do to take on such a seemingly impossible task?

Late in the afternoon, I asked Daniel to walk with me into the forest. We sat together on the flying-buttress-like root of a giant kapok tree. I confided in him that although I wanted to help, I felt inadequate and overwhelmed by my work with the Shuar. I mentioned that although I thought it was my duty to end the injustices of Big Oil, I feared retribution. I told him about the Petroecuador man and the US customs officials.

He considered what I'd said for a long moment. "I understand," he responded at last. "But there must be a way. I'll bet you know someone who could help you. Someone who could put together the partnership the Achuar want." He stopped to watch a bright blue butterfly alight on a nearby branch. "Someone who's not as vulnerable as you, who has never been in your former business, never pissed off the government, never met President Roldós." He paused. "Maybe someone who knows how to raise money."

Lynne Twist immediately came to mind. "Yes," I replied. "I do know such a person. But she'll never agree. She's way too busy with another big project—ending world hunger."

"You might be surprised." He stood up. "After all, you wrote the book *The World Is As You Dream It*. At least you can let the Achuar here know that you've come up with a possibility."

I asked Ehud for his advice.

"It seems to me," he said, "that everything you've done all your life leads to this."

That night I sat among the assembled Achuar. I knew what I had to say, but I felt very anxious. I was sure that Lynne would refuse me. How will I feel then? I asked myself. You'll feel rejected and like a failure, came the response. I hated that thought. I feared it. Feared the idea of being rejected and failing. By expressing those fears to myself, I understood that I had to confront that jaguar, I had to use my fear of rejection and failure to drive me to action. I stood up.

I was certain the Achuar closest to me could see me shaking as I stood in front of them. I told them that I had a plan. I admitted that it might not work but assured them I'd give it my best shot. When I sat down they applauded. One by one they came and thanked me.

The next morning, a group of Achuar men accompanied Ehud, Juan Gabriel, Daniel, and me to the ridge above where the permanent dock was to be built. Their faces were painted in geometric symbols and they wore red and yellow feathered crowns. One of them presented me with the serpent-headed spear he'd shaken in my face that first night. "Arutam," he said. "To protect you when you touch the jaguar."

I took it. The shaft was warm from his touch and the sun; it felt firm and strong. I made a silent vow. I'd do whatever I could to protect this land and the people who had served as its custodians for so many lifetimes, this place that had become such an integral part of my life. I placed the spear against my heart. I knew that the Arutam of those Achuar warriors was merging with the invisible darts a Shuar shaman had planted in me.

As we descended the muddy bank, I stopped to watch a family of monkeys cavort in the trees across the river. Several carried their babies on their backs. I thought about my own daughter in the US. The prospect of joining with the Achuar to create a new dream that would ensure that these forests survived for future generations brought an involuntary smile to my face. For the first time in a long time I was filled with hope.

At the urging of several of the elders, we had decided to visit a renowned Achuar shaman, a friend of Daniel's named Taish, on our way back to the airstrip. "Take ayahuasca with him," one of the elders said to me. "The plant will tell you something important." They advised us that his community had recently been attacked by another group of Achuar who believed Taish had used black magic to kill one of its shamans. However, we were assured, the troubles now were over. "Taish has great Arutam. It's a good time to share his ayahuasca." Throughout the years, following the advice of the shamans, I take ayahuasca only when I feel I have fully processed the last experience with the plant and have some new and important challenge, illness, or issue to deal with. It had been four years; I felt it was time again.

The canoe that carried us up the river was a large one. At the beginning of our journey, we had a couple dozen passengers and were loaded with many baskets of various goods. We frequently put ashore to drop people off at paths into the forest. All these men and women worked at the Kapawi site and returned home periodically to bring supplies and help with hunting, gardening, and other family chores.

The further we went, the shyer people became. At first it was only the children who ran into the forest as soon as they spotted us. Then it was the older people too. Once we passed a certain point, everyone hid from us. Daniel explained that those who had not seen outsiders before were terrified by our appearance. "Remember the Legend of the Evias,'" he asked me, "the great white cannibals who attacked the Shuar?" I did remember it as a tale that was told to the children at night, much as kids in my day had been entertained and scared with stories about boogeymen and Hansel and Gretel's wicked old witch. "The Achuar have the same legend. Maybe they think we're Evias."

I wondered if it might also have something to do with the war that had been waged against Taish.

Shortly before sunset, an impressively large oval house appeared high on a hill overlooking the river. Like both Shuar and Achuar homes, it was topped with an intricately thatched and steeply sloping roof. Like Shuar homes, but unlike other Achuar ones, it had walls constructed of vertical chonta wood poles—the same extremely strong wood they used for making spears.

"Why the walls?" I asked Daniel.

"Because they were attacked," he responded. His voice sounded tense.

As we climbed the muddy bank, I was alarmed to see Achuar warriors armed with spears—their faces heavily painted in vermillion—stationed along the trail and around the house. It was an ominous sight. I glanced back and noticed that Ehud and Juan Gabriel were still down at the river. Ehud was snapping photographs and Juan Gabriel was smoking a cigarette and chatting with several of the Achuar men. Although they seemed unconcerned, my stomach felt like a nest of writhing snakes.

"Perhaps we should go back," I whispered to Daniel.

"Let's see what Taish has to say."

A tall, muscular man, naked above the waist except for strings of beads that crisscrossed his chest, walked from the house toward us, a shotgun under one arm—an unusual and prized weapon in those days.

Every muscle in my body tightened.

He wore a traditional Achuar kilt that reached to his bare feet. His long black hair was capped with a red, yellow, black, and white feathered

---

* Sometimes spelled "Iwias"

crown. But what alarmed me most was the fierceness of his face. Two parallel red lines that crossed his cheeks and nose were connected with vermillion Xs—a symbol of the feared anaconda. More red lines ran from his ears to a mouth that was set in a stern expression. His dark eyes studied us as he approached.

Daniel stepped forward. "Hola, Taish. We come as friends," he said in Spanish.

One of the younger men moved close to Taish and translated. "You are my friend, Daniel," Taish responded. "You and your friends are welcome."

"It looks like you're still at war. Should we leave?"

"You are safe." He smiled. "Those cowards attacked me when I was alone. I sent them running. Now I have warriors at my side; they won't come near." He patted the shotgun.

When Ehud and Juan Gabriel arrived, Daniel and I explained the situation to them. They had already heard all about it from the men at the river.

"We've been assured that everything is quiet now," Juan Gabriel said.

"I think it's a great place for ayahuasca," Ehud added. "I'm for staying."

I had fasted all day, as I always did before drinking ayahuasca. From past experience, I knew that the plant would dictate what to teach me, that ultimately I would surrender to whatever came my way. However, throughout the day my thoughts often turned to the current world situation. I hoped the ayahuasca would help me gain insights into how humans had moved from lives that were simple and close to nature, like those of the Achuar, to the complex, highly materialistic, and unsustainable lives the majority of us now lead. Late in the afternoon, I walked into the forest, sat under a large kapok tree, and reviewed my life: growing up in Tilton, New Hampshire; attending college; joining the Peace Corps; becoming an EHM; working with the Shuar and Dream Change, and for SWEC. The question kept arising: Why had human beings chosen a path of cultural evolution that led to crowded cities, pollution, extreme waste, and income inequalities and that ultimately seemed destined to end in self-destruction?

I became aware that the shadows had lengthened. It was time.

I returned to Taish's home to find Daniel, Juan Gabriel, Ehud, and several Achuar men and women sitting on wooden stools in a U shape that opened to two empty stools facing each other that I knew had been placed there for the shaman. I sat next to Daniel.

"Some of Taish's family and neighbors will also drink tonight," he whispered.

Soon, Taish joined us. He was dressed as he had been earlier, in an ankle-length kilt and feathered crown, except strings of beads no longer covered his bare chest. His face was painted in the now-familiar vermillion anaconda symbol. Instead of the shotgun, he carried a large gourd and a smaller clay cup. He walked to the empty stool that faced into the U, sat down, and glanced around our group of Achuar and foreigners. His eyes met mine. For the briefest moment I thought he smiled. Then his eyes moved on.

Without saying a word, he lifted the gourd to his lap and began to whistle over it. He did this for perhaps five minutes. Then he motioned to me. I would be the first.

I stood, stepped to the empty stool, and sat down facing him. His eyes scanned me without connecting with mine. I watched as he slowly poured the thick dark liquid from the gourd into the cup, the familiar and acrid smell making me already feel the urge to vomit. He bent his head over the cup, chanted into it, and held it out to me.

I knew that my best bet was to drink it all down in one gulp—get it over with as quickly as possible. When finished, I handed the cup back to Taish and returned to my stool. I sat watching the others, one by one, repeat the same process. By the time the last Achuar had drunk his cupful, my stomach was gurgling and turning inside out. I rose from my stool and staggered outside the lodge to the edge of the forest where I dropped to my hands and knees and vomited. Foul tasting, dark orange liquid violently erupted from my mouth. I heard a voice reminding me that my body was ridding itself of bad energy. I just wanted the excruciating eruptions to end, but they went on and on.

When finally they stopped, I was exhausted. I moved from kneeling to a sitting position, with my back against a tree, and stared into the dark forest. I saw the beads of colored lights that had come to me on previous ayahuasca journeys and geometric forms that constantly shifted their shapes. After a while, I noticed shadows moving through the forest. Lots of them, weaving in and out of the trees. Men. Their naked bodies were painted red. As they approached, they waved spears toward me and Taish's lodge. Warriors. Attacking us! I was terrified. Taish's enemies had picked this most vulnerable moment to kill us all. I needed to race to the lodge and warn the others, but I was paralyzed, frozen to the spot where I sat.

Taish started chanting; everything changed.

I saw myself entering a protective bluish globe, a sort of blue haze, and rising from where I sat. Up above the canopy I went. As I looked down, the naked attackers transformed into soldiers wearing armor, metal helmets, and breastplates. They carried shields and steel swords. I was hovering over them, looking down, an observer. They led me to a Roman coliseum. From above, I watched lions mauling a group of defenseless men, women, and children. This faded to another scene: A long line of chained African slaves were whipped and beaten as they were marched from a sailing ship into a marketplace that could have been Charleston, South Carolina, or Cartagena, Colombia, in the 1700s. What followed were scene after scene of men brutalizing their fellow human beings, all the way to mammoth aircraft carriers and men piloting drones. After a while, I was witnessing a different type of horror: huge bulldozers and oil rigs ravaging the earth, gigantic factories belching pollution into the atmosphere, women prostituting themselves on street corners, massive stores where shoppers never looked at or spoke to each other, slums on the hillsides above shining glass and steel skyscrapers, families living in cardboard boxes next to open sewers, homeless people wrapped in filthy blankets beneath elevated highways, and opulent mansions high above beautiful beaches.

Again, a sudden change. I was floating across green hills, above a group of women. One of them looked up at me and pointed. "You see, the rich always want to get richer, consolidate their power," she shouted to me.

The others chimed in, a chorus: "Technology, control. Tame nature."

The leader continued with a monologue about how the rich and powerful strive to dominate everything—people and nature. In doing so, they are destroying life as we know it. "Commercialism," she said, "for them became a way of life, *the* way of life. We call them the 'faithless dominators.'"

The chorus chimed in from time to time with the refrain: "Technology, control," "faithless dominators," and "tame nature, tame nature." Finally, the leader waved me away. "You understand," she said. "Now you can return to your other world where you have work to do."

And then it was over. I found myself lying on the ground outside Taish's home. I tried to process the journey I'd just taken. It occurred to me that I had been presented with an answer to that question about why we humans had evolved into cultures that separated us from nature and were taking us down a path to self-destruction. As a species, we had marched along a path to gain more control, power, materialistic wealth, and cultural superiority. Colonialism was a hallmark of our history.

Cautiously, I rose to my knees, took several deep breaths, and stood up. I was unsteady on my feet but made my way inside to Taish, who was standing beside the fire. We stared into each other's eyes for a brief moment. He pointed to where I had laid out my sleeping bag. I bowed to him and stumbled to it. As I crawled in, I was surprised to find that Ehud, Juan Gabriel, and Daniel were lying near me, already asleep. Glancing at my watch, I was amazed to see that it was nearly midnight, more than five hours since I'd drunk the ayahuasca.

The next morning, I awoke to the sound of laughter. Looking around, I saw Ehud, Juan Gabriel, and Daniel sitting with Taish and several other Achuar men, drinking chicha. The Achuar men were laughing. I got up and joined them. Taish stood and spoke to me, Spanish words many Achuar know: "Bien. Muy bien." (Good. Very good.)

I repeated the words and then thanked him in Achuar, "Makate."

We all exchanged a few pleasantries and then continued drinking chicha and eating bananas and boiled manioc. In keeping with a post-ayahuasca custom, we briefly described our experiences.

Taish smiled when I'd finished with mine. "A large jaguar stands in front of you," he said. "And that is good because it gives you the gift of Arutam."

Before leaving Kapawi, Daniel had arranged over short-wave radio for a plane to pick us up, weather permitting, at the landing strip nearest Taish. Clouds were drifting in and we had to move quickly before the rain came. We excused ourselves, packed our gear, and headed for the canoe.

When we reached the narrow beach beside the river, Daniel hugged Juan Gabriel, Ehud, and me. He would stay behind to continue his work with the Achuar and on the Kapawi Lodge.

I took a last look around at the forest, the river, and the Achuar. These men who had defied the outside world for so many centuries realized something that was vitally important. They had to touch their jaguar, confront their greatest fear. I understood that, as the woman who had visited me in the night had said, I had work to do. I had to confront the faithless dominators and find people from my world who would help the Achuar move us out of our "tame nature" mind-set. And I had to overcome my fear of rejection and failure.

I stepped into the dugout canoe and, along with Ehud and Juan Gabriel and four Achuar men, headed for the airstrip.

One of the Achuar men came and sat next to me. "My ancestors appeared to me last night during the ayahuasca ceremony," he said in Spanish, pointing at the sky. "They are up there. Los Sabios watch over us and send advice. They told me that you and your people will help us protect our lands from the oil companies. And we must teach your people about taking care of everything that takes care of us—the plants, the rivers, and the animals.

As we continued down the river, the words of that woman in my ayahuasca journey returned to me: "Commercialism . . . *the* way of life . . . faithless dominators . . . you have work to do." It seemed I'd been given a mandate to create a plan my world would understand. But what exactly was the work I had to do?

17

FACING A JAGUAR

AFTER LANDING AT THE SMALL AIRPORT we'd flown out of days earlier at the edge of the jungle, the three of us took the jeep Juan Gabriel had left there to Quito, and three days after leaving Kapawi, I arrived at Miami International Airport.

Once again, I was strip searched by customs officials. It was degrading and deeply upsetting, but this time, rather than intimidated, I felt angry. As those two men roughly frisked my naked body, I realized that I was just getting a small dose of what it must be like to be an immigrant or a non-white US citizen, discriminated against and maltreated by representatives of a powerful government. I had a renewed determination to stand up to a system that exploits and abuses the defenseless.

As I drove north to my house in Palm Beach Gardens, my thoughts switched from that customs experience back to the Amazon and then to my upcoming call with Lynne Twist. The anxiety I'd felt in that Achuar lodge returned. She'll be insulted, I told myself. I could hear her voice, as though she were sitting beside me in my car: Didn't you listen to what I said about my commitment to the Hunger Project? or How can you even ask such a thing?

By the time I arrived home, I'd convinced myself to delay even thinking about calling her until the next morning.

Over dinner, my wife, Winifred, asked me to tell her all about the trip. When I did, I could not avoid including my nervousness around Lynne.

"What will you do if she doesn't agree to help?" Winifred asked.

"I don't know. But I'll probably never be able to show my face in Ecuador again." We both laughed. I'd said it in jest; however, as I tried to fall asleep later that night, I was haunted by the thought that it might be true.

The next morning came far too quickly. I went to my office and stared at the phone—one of the first cordless models. And the clock. It was 9:30 a.m. East Coast time. Whew! Only 6:30 a.m. in California, where Lynne lived. Too early to call her.

I went through the stack of mail on my desk and paid a bunch of bills.

Then it was 11 a.m., already 8 a.m. in California. I knew that Lynne was often on the phone by 7:30 a.m.

I decided to have a second cup of coffee before calling her. I needed that extra jolt of caffeine.

Sitting at my desk, sipping coffee as slowly as I could, looking at a painting on the wall of an Ecuadorian street scene, I worried about what I'd tell Daniel when Lynne refused me. How would he explain my failure to the Achuar? What would I say to Ehud, the publisher of my books?

Then I saw the irony of those two questions. One dealt with a culture that was under severe threats from foreign companies, the other with personal pride.

A memory came to me of eighth grade, walking across a gymnasium, and asking a girl to dance. She turned me down. A gymnasium full of people was watching, judging, sniggering behind my back . . . At least that's what I'd felt.

I set my coffee mug down, closed my eyes, and tried to meditate. But thoughts kept bubbling up around my fear of rejection and failure. It had been a factor in so much of my life. And yet. In my earlier career I had been extremely successful at convincing leaders of countries to accept the EHM deals I offered. If at first they refused, I kept at them. What was the difference?

I was standing before that eighth-grade girl, feeling vulnerable, exposed, naked. I was seated at a conference table with powerful men, papers spread out on the table in front of me—feeling competent, confident, well dressed in my business suit armor.

From those two images, I realized that the gymnasium episode had been personal. I'd made myself vulnerable to that girl—and a gym full of my classmates—and she'd turned me down. Rejected me. Me. Personally. On the other hand, the EHM deals were not about me. Not personal. That difference had marked my life.

The fear of personal rejection, being judged, vulnerable to the opinion of others was one of my jaguars. Lynne Twist would turn me down. Me.

I opened my eyes. The serpent-headed spear that the Achuar had given me was lying on the desk in front of me. Arutam.

I was being called upon to transform my fear of rejection and failure into action.

I picked up the spear and felt its firmness, its strength. I laid the point against my forehead, my third eye, and then my heart. If she turned me down, it was because of her commitment to the Hunger Project. Not a rejection of me.

I set the spear down next to the phone and dialed Lynne's number.

She answered almost immediately. "Thank God you're there." I could hear her sigh with relief. "I've been trying to call you. You never answer. Your answering machine kept saying that you were away and it was full."

I released a long breath. "I was in Ecuador. Why were you calling me?"

"I just got back from Africa where I had the strangest experience. It's got me worried, scared. I hoped you could help me."

She explained that while she was in Ghana, at a Hunger Project meeting, visions like those she had experienced in Guatemala returned.

"As I sat at that table with all those African men, their faces morphed into ones that were painted with geometric designs; they wore red and yellow feathered crowns around their heads. I excused myself, went to the ladies' room, and tried to recompose myself. But when I returned to the meeting, it happened again. I told them I was ill, excused myself from the meeting, packed my bags, and took the next flight home to San Francisco." She paused. I could hear her breathing. "But," she continued, her voice filled with anxiety, "the visions persist. They've totally disrupted my life! I don't know what to make of them. I figured you might be able to help, given your experiences with shamans."

I could barely believe what I was hearing. I wanted to shout it out, but I forced myself to stay calm. "The Achuar," I said into the telephone. "You saw the Achuar."

"What?"

"The Amazonian people I just visited." I was now on my feet, holding the phone up to my ear, walking around the room—bouncing around the room. "They're calling you." There was silence on the wires that stretched across the continent. I couldn't help giving a little laugh. "Do you remember, when we were in Guatemala, I told you about the belief that you must 'touch the jaguar'?"

"I think so." Another pause. "Yes. It's about confronting the things we fear."

"Well . . ." I was determined not to sound like a child who's just been given carte blanche in a candy store. "They reminded me that, when we touch the jaguar, we understand our fears and the obstacles that hold us back. We don't run from them; instead, we face them and change our perceptions of them. Then we take the actions necessary to change ourselves and our societies. They told me during this past trip that we are the thing they most fear, our oil companies, our way of life, our extreme materialism. They said they had dreamed on this, that their shamans had gone deep into the meaning of their visions, and they had concluded that they have to touch us—their people have to touch our people—initiate contact with the very thing they most fear."

"The modern world . . ."

"Exactly." I couldn't hold back my enthusiasm. "Yes, that's exactly it! That's exactly what they said."

"Amazing. So they came to you . . ."

"To my friend Daniel, and then me."

"People they trust."

"They want to learn about the modern world, our world, so they can be prepared for major contact when it comes. Defend themselves against the oil companies. They asked me to help them."

"The Prophecy of the Eagle and the Condor." She let out a long breath. "And?"

"I told them I'd find someone better suited than me to facilitate this." I waited for her to ask the obvious question.

She was silent.

"You." More silence. "You have the ideal background through your fundraising, philanthropic, and networking activities and your experiences with people in Africa, India, and now Guatemala. I was so impressed by the way you organized the Katalysis trip. I told the Achuar that you might be willing to put together a group of people who could form a partnership with them. Their people and ours. They got very excited, enthusiastic, and told me to invite you to come to them—with such a group. It was more than an invitation. They said it is ordained."

PART 6

THE LEGEND OF THE EVIAS

1994–1995

You must ask yourself about the Evias in your life. What scares you? . . . What must you do to change this? . . . You must do this alone. No one can help you. Only by doing that will you avoid going to war with yourself.

18

STEALING A COUNTRY

When the invitation, or really the "call," came from the remote, indig-
enous people deep in the Amazon, it was a call I could not deny.
So John and I helped organize a group of twelve travelers from the
modern world to meet with the Achuar leaders. The group was com-
posed of people of enormous quality and integrity—people with open
hearts, each of whom had a global voice of some kind in their own
issue, and some understanding of the importance of the rain forest
to the sustainability of all life. These were people with the humility
to be open to indigenous wisdom, who would respect the ways of the
shaman and the way of life in the Achuar community.[1]

—Lynne Twist, *The Soul of Money*

LYNNE AGREED DURING THAT PHONE CALL to do what the Achuar had
requested. Immediately afterward, she began to draw up a list of people
who might be interested and who had the networks and skills required to
create a partnership like the one the Achuar wanted. We began to contact
them. However, politics interfered. Tensions between Ecuador and Peru
during 1994 over a disputed area in the rain forest, followed by a brief
border war in early 1995, delayed us for more than a year, until a peace
treaty between the two countries was signed. After that, the two of us
resumed our efforts at contacting the people on Lynne's list.

We had our work cut out for us. Every one of them had heard about the border war. We had to convince them that it truly was over. In addition, we needed to warn them of the hardships and potential dangers of a journey into the rain forests of the Amazon. They were about to be the first outsiders that many of the Achuar had ever seen. They would be living in primitive conditions. They would canoe down rivers that were home to caimans and anacondas and walk through forests inhabited by jaguars, wild boars, and poisonous snakes. There would be no hot water, no toilets, no soft beds, and no bellhops to handle their luggage. They would sleep under mosquito netting in sleeping bags that they would have to carry with them.

We knew that we had to address all these things. I personally felt very conflicted. Although I understood the importance of defining all the potential problems, I did not want to discourage anyone from coming. I desperately wanted something significant to happen on this trip. I had no idea what that might look like; the word the Achuar had used—"partnership"—was the best I could find. But, what did that mean?

In a series of phone calls and letters, Lynne and I advised each of them of the discomforts, hardships, and dangers. But beyond that, we also emphasized the historical significance of this trip and the beauty of the place. I told them the rivers they would canoe down were home to beautiful and playful freshwater dolphins and the forests were inhabited by brilliantly colored macaws, toucans, and butterflies and home to cavorting monkeys. They would have the opportunity to stay in the home of a shaman honored and respected by his people and, we believed, take ayahuasca and receive a healing from him. They would get to mingle with men, women, and children who had invited them into their communities because they wanted to form a partnership that would change human attitudes toward the rain forests and perhaps even the very nature of our presence on this planet. Ecuador and Peru were at peace. This trip would, I promised, be the adventure of a lifetime.

There was one added point that I believe raised the confidence of at least some of them. I was able to tell them that my twelve-year-old daughter, Jessica, was going with us. Winifred and I had first taken her to visit the Mayan lands of Mexico when she was less than a year old and, since then, had taken her several times to the Ecuadorian Andes. Although she had never been to the Amazon, she was excited by the idea and both Winifred and I thought it would be a good experience for her. I have no doubt that knowing that Jessica would travel with us helped our invitees feel more confident that I would do everything possible to keep them out of harm's way.

In the end we had twelve people, in addition to our two Ecuadorian guides, Daniel and Juan Gabriel: Ella Allford; Dave Ellis; Trish Waldron; Deb Emmershien; Jim Gollin; Bob Graham; Wendy Graham; Josh Mailman; Lynne Twist and her husband, Bill; Jessica; and me. Some of us met at the Miami airport; the rest flew directly to Quito.

That journey to Achuar Territory in 1995 took us in our modern air-conditioned rented bus from Quito, over the top of the Andes, down to the jungle. Although the bus was a huge contrast from the wooden box of twenty-seven years earlier, the muddy serpentine road was a reminder of those days. Yet, perhaps because of the comforts on that bus, the people seemed to find the trip to be a grand adventure with breath-taking views of the Pastaza River canyon.

Sheer cliffs rose up on one side, like the walls of a huge fortress punctured by the blazing arrows of crimson bromeliads. Every couple of miles or so, a cascading waterfall drenched our bus. On the other side, the earth tumbled abruptly into a deep abyss; at the bottom, the Pastaza River snaked toward its union with the Amazon.

Across the Pastaza, the landscape changed. Steep slopes, once lush with tropical forests, were destroyed and scarred—laid barren by the greed of oil and lumber companies and the farmers who followed once those companies built roads. As I stared through the window at the devastation, these scenes evoked memories of Ecuador in 1968.

Despite Texaco's claims that petroleum was a miracle that would catapult an impoverished nation into prosperity, the miracle had turned into a nightmare. The scenes we were now witnessing reflected the irony of modern economics. Vast forests had been destroyed as oil company roads opened the jungle to colonization and development. Macaws, jaguars, monkeys, tapirs, and Indigenous cultures had been driven deeper into the forest. A little further north, the oil companies had turned the once pristine rivers into burning chemical cesspools, and local residents suffered from extremely high rates of cancer and childhood leukemia. Throughout the entire region, people who'd been told they would prosper from "development" desperately struggled to survive.

At one point along the road, we came in sight of the mammoth cement wall of the Agoyan hydroelectric dam. Daniel spoke into the microphone. "I think John has a few words to say about this dam."

Slowly I pulled myself out of my seat. As I stepped forward, I fought back my emotions and tried to calm the conflicting feelings about how much I should share with these people.

Daniel handed me the microphone. He told the driver to stop. We pulled off the road at a spot that gave us an unencumbered view of that vast gray wall.

"Well," I said, "it's part of my story as an economic consultant . . ." I studied the microphone in my hand. What the hell! "The nickname we used for ourselves was economic hit man." It was the first time I'd spoken those words in public. I briefly summarized my work. "Here in Ecuador," I continued, "we focused on building electrical systems." I pointed through the window. "Although this dam wasn't completed until the 1980s, the planning began during the '60s. After a coup in 1972, the new dictator, General Lara, a graduate of the School of the Americas, the CIA's man in Ecuador, agreed to World Bank and Inter-American Development Bank loans to build dams and other infrastructure. US companies made millions off the very lucrative engineering and construction contracts they were able to negotiate with often-corrupt Ecuadorian officials. A few wealthy Ecuadorians, those who owned energy-dependent factories and other businesses, became superrich. But the bad news: funds for education, health care, and other social services that helped everyone else were ransacked to pay interest on the debt. One of the conditions of the loans was that Ecuador would allow Texaco and other oil companies to expand their operations deeper into the rain forests." I glanced at the faces on that bus. "It was pure colonialism," I said. "The US was building an empire—in Asia, the Middle East, Latin America, and parts of Africa. Today we have less than 5 percent of the world's population and consume more than 20 percent of its resources."

"How do you define 'colonialism' and 'empire'?" a woman at the back of the bus asked.

"Colonialism," I replied, "occurs when a country moves in on another country or culture and takes control of its economy, lands, resources, people, and system of government. There are a number of characteristics of an empire, but the big five are it has colonized many other countries or cultures; its people consume a disproportionate amount of resources per capita; its language is accepted as the standard, used in commerce and politics; its money is the predominate currency; and its military is huge and ready to protect the empire's interests everywhere.

"Sounds like the United States today," a man said.

All I could do was nod my head in agreement and fight back the emotions that silenced me.

Several people moaned.

"You've returned to redeem yourself," the woman at the back of the bus observed.

Daniel told the driver to continue. The bus lurched forward. I lost my balance. Daniel caught me.

"The dam strikes back," I said as I recovered my balance.

People laughed, a welcome relief.

"Tell them about Roldós," Daniel urged.

"Here's a significant story," I said. "Democratic elections were held in 1978, after a long period of CIA-supported dictators. A lawyer named Jaime Roldós, who'd run on a platform to rein in the oil companies and force them to clean up the pollution they caused and share a portion of their profits with Ecuadorians, won the presidency. I was sent here, along with other EHMs, to convince Roldós to change his ways, not to honor his promises—using both the carrot of financial rewards and the stick of CIA threats, coups, and assassinations." Words caught in my throat. I stood there, again unable to speak.

Daniel took the microphone from me. "President Roldós died when his private plane crashed."

I leaned into the microphone. "I'm quite certain he was assassinated." I looked out at them. "Enough for now."

I sat down next to Jessica.

"Good job, Dad." She patted my leg.

I spent the rest of the ride staring quietly out the window. I could hear the others talking about what I'd said. I knew they had questions. But I was in no mood to talk more about these dark aspects of my life and my country, and they seemed to understand. Finally, we arrived in Shell, a town formed around an airstrip built by the oil company of the same name and used by the Ecuadorian military as headquarters for its Amazonian operations—and by mercenaries to protect oil company operations.

We clambered off the bus and gathered together in one of the hangars, waiting to fly into another dirt airstrip that was newer than the one where I'd landed on my previous trip and that was located in a community where Kichwa and Shuar people live that was closer to Kapawi.

While we waited, I spoke to the group about something that been increasingly on my mind since my last trip to visit the Achuar. I told them that they were about to meet people who lived as most humans had for nearly all our history. "We've been around for roughly two hundred thousand years," I said, "And during all but the last three to four thousand years our ancestors lived in close harmony with nature. Their lifestyles—their economies—emphasized taking care of their children and their children's children and many generations into the future. The people you're about to meet want you here because they understand that our modern ways of living—our economies—are based on short-term, greedy, and ultimately self-destructive perceptions. They've seen the terrible devastation that's hit their Indigenous neighbors as a result of oil development and the roads, pipelines, labor camps, and other infrastructure the companies construct. They want us to leave here inspired to take a message to the modern world that we must change, we must stop the destruction."

"That's all so true," Daniel added. "And I also want to mention that some of the non-Achuar people in the community we will walk through are jealous of the fact that we're building a lodge with the Achuar that's a fair distance from their community. They wanted it to be closer to them, on a much less attractive site. Don't be surprised if they're not too friendly."

19

PIRANHAS

TO ACCOMMODATE ALL OF US, our luggage, and the supplies we'd need during our days in the jungle, we had rented three small planes. Before we left home, Winifred had insisted that father and daughter fly on separate ones. She didn't have faith in small planes and wanted to make sure that if one went down both of us would not be on it. Daniel divided the three groups accordingly. Jessica joined him on the first plane. I was on the second, and Juan Gabriel, Lynne, and Bill were on the third.

Flying over that vast rain forest, I was excited to return to this land I loved. Then my mind started overacting. I became apprehensive that something would go wrong. A plane would crash. The Kichwa would turn violent. A canoe would capsize and someone would drown. I couldn't shake my fear that the Achuar dream of partnership would become a nightmare.

After about an hour in the air, I spotted a cut in the jungle, a long narrow patch of dirt amidst the trees—our landing strip. As the pilot circled, I peered down and was greatly relieved to see Jessica, Daniel, and their group disembarking their plane. They were safe!

We landed and our two groups had an emotional reunion. Jessica threw her arms around me. "These forests are so huge, so vast, so beautiful," she gushed as we embraced each other.

Together with four Achuar men, our groups unloaded our planes. While we gathered our equipment and began strapping on our backpacks, one of the pilots rushed up to us. He looked worried.

"I talked by radio with the pilot of the third plane." He gestured frantically at the distant sky that was overhung with dark clouds. "Bad weather forced it down." He crossed himself.

"Are they OK?" Daniel asked.

"I think so. They landed at a missionary airstrip."

Our people huddled around us, concerned expressions on their faces. Everyone was looking up to where the pilot had pointed; the ominous clouds were moving rapidly toward us.

"Did something happen to Bill and Lynne?" someone asked.

"Should we go back and find them?" another added.

"It's OK." Daniel explained what had happened. "Weather often forces planes to land at alternate airstrips." He managed a smile. "As soon as it clears, they'll join us."

I wished I could share his confidence.

He took the Achuar men aside and conferred quietly with them. Then he came back to us. "Let's go ahead to the lodge. We can set things up before it gets dark."

He led us along a trail that took us to the nearby community. As we trudged past the thatched roofs of the homes in the community where, Daniel had warned, people might be upset that we were building a lodge that wasn't closer to them, it seemed that we had entered a ghost town. No one greeted us. Not a person in sight anywhere. A couple of mangy dogs stood in doorways, bared their teeth, and growled at us. Otherwise, no sign of life. It was odd, rare, and disturbing. Never before had I experienced anything like this in an Indigenous community.

Sweat trickled down my face, my arms—my entire body—and it wasn't just from the tropical heat.

"Damn," Daniel muttered. "The people here don't get that we're trying to protect them and their jungle, as well as those of the Achuar who are building the lodge. A long history of exploitation has made them suspicious of outsiders." I sensed that he suspected something was not right.

"Seems hostile," I replied.

He nodded. "They're watching us, but we can't see them."

Finally, we put the community behind us. We trudged on for another ten minutes or so, along a jungle trail, before arriving at the Pastaza River.

It was wider here than it had been at the location where I'd first seen it months before, about as wide as the length of a football field, and even more turbulent than before. The memory of that earlier day, the threats against my Shuar friend, Yahanua, came back to me.

I stepped away from the group and stood alone, looking out at those seething waters and the menacing dark clouds that were now nearly above us, and I thought about Yahanua and about Bill and Lynne's group. A nest of gnarled branches bobbed and spun near the middle of the river, like the matted hair of a giant's submerged head. Suddenly it disappeared into a whirlpool. Within seconds it reappeared, fifty feet or more down the river. Hurled skyward, it hung suspended and then plummeted back into the foaming current. I wondered what Yahanua would say. Would she see the violence of this river as an omen? The nest of branches as a symbol for the third plane—or our entire group?

The black clouds, the seething river, the oppressive atmosphere brought Joseph Conrad's *Heart of Darkness* to mind. Was I, like Conrad's Kurtz, the station manager for a European ivory company in the nineteenth-century Congo, ushering into this land the darkness, cruelty, and barbarism of what Conrad sarcastically referred to as "civilization"? It was a term that to him was just an excuse for colonizing people with resources England coveted. I too was bringing in people from a country with a long record of violence toward Indigenous people. Could what I was doing somehow result in more damage and suffering? Were my attempts at redemption about to plunge me—and these other people, Achuar and Americans alike—deeper into the darkness?

"John!" It was Daniel. He was waving frantically for me to join him and the rest of the group near a large dugout canoe.

I walked along the river bank, trying to shake the dark thoughts from my mind, reminding myself that we were here because the Achuar had invited us to partner with them. Yet, I could not obliterate the image of that lonely, desperate, and abandoned man, Kurtz. Or the haunting last words of Marlon Brando who played his equivalent in *Apocalypse Now*, a modernized movie adaptation about the US's attempts to colonize Vietnam. "The horror," Brando mumbled as he lay dying. And repeated, "The horror."

When I reached Daniel, he was standing beside the canoe. Everyone else was seated in it, staring at the churning water, making no attempt to disguise their anxieties.

I climbed into the canoe. Daniel sat beside me in the bow. He pointed at another canoe pulled up on the bank further down the river and a couple of men standing near it. "They're from that community we passed through," he said.

"The hostile one?"

"Yes, but they weren't there. They just returned from fishing. I paid them to bring Bill and Lynne's group as soon as they land."

"Do you trust them?"

"Money talks. Even here in the jungle." He stood up, steadying himself with a hand on my shoulder, and turned to face the others. "This too is the Pastaza," he yelled in a voice that rose above the roar of the rushing water. "It looks a lot different, but it's the same beautiful river you saw in that canyon in the mountains." I knew it was his attempt to reassure them.

"The one dammed at Agoyan?" someone asked.

"Yes." He gave a laugh and sat down beside me.

The words rang in my ears: the one dammed at Agoyan. I'd damned that river—and myself. I'd locked myself in a cage of guilt and silence.

Daniel motioned to the Achuar man at the stern of the canoe. He began yanking on the starter cord of the ancient outboard motor. It refused to start.

All heads turned to the man at the stern.

He pulled harder. Again and again, it sputtered and died.

Another Achuar joined him. After perhaps a dozen attempts, it turned over. It sounded like a person wheezing with pneumonia. To make matters worse, it was not strong enough to pull us off the dirt.

Daniel jumped into the water and gave the canoe a shove. Slowly, the bow swung away from the shore. He climbed in and we headed out onto the river.

As we fought our way against the swift current, a gigantic tree trunk bucked and tumbled and nearly struck us.

"Must have been a big storm upriver," Daniel yelled into my ear. "These people are getting their money's worth!"

Too much of their money's worth, I thought. Tree trunks continued to come dangerously close. The dark clouds threatened a deluge like the one I remembered from the earlier trip.

As we chugged through the violent water, I could not wipe out the memory of the Agoyan dam, TV images of Roldós's crashed plane, and the terrible black lakes of oil that inundated the jungle to the north of us. Or Brando's voice: "The horror."

Then our canoe made a sharp turn and passed beneath a huge branch that arched above us. Everything changed. The river grew narrow, the water tranquil. We'd left the Pastaza. The motor slowed and everything became quieter.

Daniel stood and turned to face the others. "The Capahuari," he said, glowing. "Beautiful river for swimming. We'll be at the lodge soon."

"Any piranhas?" someone asked.

"Yes," Daniel replied. "But they're harmless. Little fish don't attack big animals like us."

I took his hand and pulled myself up beside him. It seemed like the perfect opportunity to distract people from ingrained perceptions that were scaring them. "Man-eating piranhas are a myth that, according to what I've read, started with President Teddy Roosevelt. Some Brazilians blocked off a section of a river and left a bunch of piranhas there for many days without food. When Roosevelt arrived, they led him to the side of the river and pushed in a cow or a goat. The starving fish went into a feeding frenzy. Later Roosevelt wrote about the vicious man-eating piranhas of the Amazon."

"Are you sure about that?" came the question.

"About them not being dangerous? Absolutely." I paused. "I have heard that if a school of them gets left stranded in a pool after a flash flood and they are starving, they may go into a feeding frenzy, as Roosevelt observed. But I've never met anyone who's witnessed it."

"I've swum with thousands of piranhas," Daniel said then added, "What you will find here that's not a myth are the beautiful freshwater pink dolphins. Hopefully, they'll join us when we go for a swim. They're very friendly."

Trees along the shore spread their branches over our canoe, sheltering us from the dark clouds. Our navigator shut down the motor and allowed us to drift so we could hear birds singing.

The people behind me began to talk with each other enthusiastically. I turned to see them as they watched a flock of chattering parrots fly overhead and white herons that were wading near the shore. Then it seemed that everyone was pointing at something: the massive trees along the banks, the brilliantly colored heliconia flowers that hung over the water, the florescent blue morpho butterflies that sometimes alighted on our canoe, and a family of howler monkeys in a nearby tree.

Once a group of naked Achuar children scrambled down mud steps cut into the steep embankment and silently watched until we turned a corner.

Then we were there—at the U-shaped bend in the Capahuari where on that earlier visit Daniel had convinced me to agree to help the Achuar. The sun was out, the clouds had disappeared as quickly as they had arrived. We were greeted by an assembly of Achuar men. Their faces painted with orange and black symbols, they were bare above the waist except for beaded necklaces, wore the traditional kilts that reached nearly to their ankles, and had yellow and red feather crowns on their heads. They helped us disembark onto a newly constructed dock. They led us along a raised boardwalk to a lone platform that had been built on poles high above a lake formed by a bend in the river; the wall-less platform was covered with a palm-frond roof. Daniel explained that eventually this would become the bar area for the lodge, but for now it would be our temporary home—a man-made island high above the water.

After giving us a tour of the area, he pointed out that it would be dark in a couple of hours. He suggested that we dig out the mosquito-net tents we'd brought and create a little community beneath the thatched roof to make it as comfortable as possible for the people in the third group once they arrived.

Things seemed to have taken a turn for the better . . . until, as Jessica and I were finishing setting up our tent, Daniel interrupted us. He took me aside. He looked worried. "I heard the third plane arrive," he said, "back when I was showing the group around, well over an hour and a half ago. They should've been here long before now."

"What do you think happened?"

"I don't know, but I had a bad feeling when we walked through that community." He paused. "I'm going to take the canoe back to find out."

"What about the Achuar guys who were with us?"

"They returned to their camp. I'll try to pick them up on the way."

"I'll come with you."

"No, no. You stay here. Don't worry these people. If they ask, tell them I was concerned that there might not have been another canoe there, so I took ours to meet Bill and Lynne and their crew." He forced a smile. "Actually, that could be the case."

But I knew he didn't believe it; we'd both seen that other canoe on the bank of the river, along with the Kichwa men he'd hired to transport our people.

20

KIDNAPPED

IN ECUADOR, a country that owes its name to the fact that it lies on the equator, the sun sets at close to 6:30 p.m. every day all year round.

As sunset approached, my nerves got the better of me. Daniel was gone. The Achuar were gone. We had no canoe and no way out. I didn't dare confide my anxiety to Jessica or anyone else. What could I do? How long should I wait before telling the rest of them the truth? What was the truth? The plane crashed? There had been violence? I only knew that Daniel had left nearly an hour and a half earlier and he'd heard the plane an hour and a half before that.

I went to Jessica and, trying to sound as if nothing bothered me, asked her to enlist the others to help her unpack the things we needed for dinner.

"What's going on, Dad?" Her voice revealed her own anxiety.

"I'm sure everything's fine."

She gave me a look. "Come on, Dad. I know you."

"OK, OK. I'm worried, but we mustn't scare the others."

"I'll do my best," she said, without pressuring me to explain more.

And I knew she would. Her cooperation buoyed me. I headed back along the boardwalk toward the dock. On the way, I passed a small tool-shed. The door was open. Leaning against an inside wall was a machete. I'd been a martial arts black belt for years. This might be the time . . . I picked up the machete and continued walking.

Suddenly I heard a sound.

The motor. The faint but familiar coughing of that old outboard on our canoe. A surge of hope . . . I headed down the boardwalk and broke into a run before realizing that I didn't know who was in the canoe. It could be the community's warriors come to kill us. I slowed as the boardwalk curved toward the dock. My grip on the machete tightened. I stopped.

In the dimming light, the bow of the canoe appeared. It had a hazy, surrealistic look as it slowly came around the bend. I knelt on one knee and stared into the shadows.

It continued toward me and the ghostly outlines of people began to emerge. One was standing in the bow waving something. A spear?

I lifted my machete.

Arms. The person standing in the bow was waving his arms.

"Hola." It was Daniel's distinctive voice.

I stood up. He was braced in the bow waving and shouting. Right behind him: Juan Gabriel, Bill, and Lynne. Waving. Now I saw more people, ours and a couple of the Achuar who'd been in our earlier canoe, behind them. Waving.

As they pulled toward the dock, I counted. All of them were there and they were shouting and laughing. I dropped the machete. Feeling as if a great weight had lifted, I ran to the end of the dock.

Daniel tossed me a rope; I helped guide the boat alongside the dock.

"We're ready for dinner," Juan Gabriel said.

"What happened?"

"Ask them." Daniel pointed at the others as he stepped onto the wooden platform.

"We were kidnapped," someone said.

I stared at Daniel. "Well, sort of." He frowned.

As we walked back toward where Jessica and the others were waiting, Daniel filled me in, with help from Bill and Lynne. Apparently, the community's leader had been out hunting when our first two groups went through his community. By the time the third flight landed, he was back. And he had drunk a lot of chicha. He insisted that they all join him in the communal meeting lodge to drink chicha. After an hour or so—and more chicha than they wanted (but did not dare refuse)—he told them that they would spend the night in his community. He pointed at a small hut that Bill described as "looking like a run-down and uncomfortable maintenance shed—something Lynne and I were not at all enthusiastic about."

Following what seemed to them like interminable hours, Daniel arrived. "Angry as hell," someone said. He assured the community that these people had come to help them—not just the Achuar but all the Amazonian nations. He made it clear that they should have been transported to the lodge and pointed out that several men had been paid to do exactly that. A heated discussion followed.

Finally, Daniel turned to the group. "Gather your things and let's get out of here," he said and led them to his own waiting canoe and some of the Achuar men he had picked up along the way.

It was a bizarre story—one of the many strange events that swirled around this entire endeavor. Someone suggested it should be made into a movie. I had a darker thought. As soon as I had the opportunity, I took Daniel aside and expressed my concern that what everyone now referred to as "the kidnapping" would sour the group on Kapawi.

"I think the leader of that community was trying to ruin everything."

"That was his objective?" I asked.

"With him, you never know. He's half Kichwa and half Shuar—traditional enemies of the Achuar. Even though people are beginning to understand that the real enemies are the oil companies, they are stuck in some of their old ways. Men like him use this to gain power."

"Does this give him power?"

"He thinks so."

"How can we make our people feel better?"

"Just wait," he said confidently. "Tonight will be special."

After dinner, he ushered the group back to the canoe. The Achuar navigator headed up the Capahuari. Daniel asked him to turn off the motor. As the dugout started to drift silently back toward the lodge, Daniel stood up. "You're going to be treated to a celestial sight few people ever witness," he said. He pointed in one direction. "There's the Southern Cross." Then he turned 180 degrees. "And there, the Big Dipper. Follow those two stars at the end of the Big Dipper and you'll see the North Star. Only on the equator are the Southern Cross and North Star visible at the same time." He went on to point out other constellations and recite some of the ancient legends around them. These included stories from Greek and Roman mythology, as well as ones from the Achuar.

Sitting there in the night, on that peaceful starlit river, Lynne shared the thrill she had felt once she was free of the community and saw the Achuar men in the canoe Daniel had brought. Their faces were the same ones that had visited her in the visions she'd experienced in Guatemala and Ghana, faces of men painted with orange and black designs and who wore yellow and red feather crowns. "I knew then," she said, "that I have to do everything I can to form a partnership with them."

Looking up into the stars that night, I took Jessica's hand in mine. I felt that we had passed some sort of initiation. I could not have known that the initiation was far from over.

21

EVIL

THE NEXT DAY, we took the group on a hike through the forest. We made frequent stops so that Daniel and one of our Achuar guides could explain the uses of various plants and trees—some for food or medicines; some for making tools, weapons, canoes, and ornaments; and still others for the construction of homes and lodges.

"The jungle provides everything," Daniel explained. "Many modern pharmaceuticals are derived from rain forest plants. One example is curare, a plant extract that Amazonian hunters smear onto the tips of their blowgun darts."

"Poison darts!" someone exclaimed.

"Safer than that," Daniel responded. "These people are smart enough not to inject poison into an animal they intend to eat. Curare paralyzes monkeys and birds so they fall out of trees. It and derivatives have been used in hospitals as part of modern anesthesia treatments for more than a hundred years."

Our Achuar guide led us to a tall tree next to the trail. When he made a small cut in its bark with his machete, a dark red liquid that looked like blood oozed out.

"Sangre de Drago," Daniel explained. "The perfect antiseptic." He glanced around. "Who's got a cut?"

One of the women stepped forward. "A scratch," she said, holding out her arm.

Daniel picked up a small stick, scraped a patch of the red liquid onto his finger, and massaged it into her cut. It turned, as if by magic, into a white cream.

"Already feels better," she laughed. "Amazing."

"Better than peroxide," Daniel observed. "Anyone got mosquito bites?"

For the next few minutes Daniel administered Sangre de Drago to several people. As he did so, one of the men recalled the talk I'd given in the airplane hangar about people living in harmony with nature. "We sure see that here," he said. "It sounded quaint, almost unbelievable, back there, just a couple days ago. Now, it's real. Makes you wonder how we can be so greedy, so stupid, and unconscious of the mess we're leaving for our children."

We continued walking and within an hour arrived at a clearing that was planted with manioc bushes. "A sign we're approaching an Achuar community," Daniel explained. "This is one of their most important plants. A basic food and also what the women use to make chicha."

Our Achuar guide spoke to Daniel, who interpreted. "You're the first group from the outside to visit this community. They've only seen two other white men—a priest and me. No women. A runner this morning let them know we're coming; they're expecting us, but we are a novelty."

"I'm going to run ahead," Jessica told me. "I want to film everyone walking in." My twelve-year-old daughter had brought what was considered at the time a state-of-the-art camcorder. A telephoto zoom lens protruded from it. When she held the camera to her eye, all that was visible above her neck was a mouth filled with braces that sparkled in the sunlight, the lens, and her long flowing light brown hair.

"OK." I said. "Just don't get too far ahead."

She raced down the narrow jungle trail and disappeared around a corner.

The rest of us continued walking. No one said a word. Everyone's attention was focused on the significance of being the first group of outsiders and the first foreign women to enter this community.

Suddenly Jessica reappeared. She was racing back toward us, the camcorder jerking madly from a strap at her side. Tears streamed down her cheeks.

Daniel and I ran to her. Daniel got there first and knelt down to embrace her. "What's wrong?" he asked. "Are you hurt?"

"They called me 'evil,'" she sobbed. "Why would they call me 'evil'?"

I glanced at Daniel. He shrugged. "The Achuar don't speak English," he said. "Who's there in that community? Who called you 'evil'?"

People began to gather around us; the word "evil" hung in the air.

Jessica fought to catch her breath. "The children," she said at last. "When they saw me, they shouted 'evil' and ran away, into the forest."

By now everyone had caught up to us. I glanced at their tense faces. This was it. If the "kidnapping" hadn't ended the possibility of partnership, this surely would.

Then I heard Daniel. He was quietly laughing.

I looked at him.

"It's OK," he said, peering into Jessica's tear-streaked eyes. "That's the word you heard, but they weren't saying that." He scrutinized the people standing around and gave another reassuring laugh. "Those kids referred to the 'Evias.' Mythological beings." Then to me, "You explain, John. It's the same as for the Shuar."

Of course! Why hadn't I thought of that?

I stood up and helped my daughter to her feet. Several women wrapped their arms around Jessica. I briefly summarized a legend about giant white cannibals who came out of the deep forest to eat the Shuar and Achuar and their children. "I'll go into more details later," I promised. "It's a particularly interesting legend these days, because some of the Shuar and Achuar who are fighting against the onslaught of oil say that the companies are a modern manifestation of the Evias." I turned to Jessica. "When you went into the community, were you filming?"

"Yes," she answered, dabbing at her tears with a handkerchief that had been handed to her. "I was so excited. I saw a group of kids and ran toward them pointing my camera. I wanted to show them playing before you guys entered and then film their reactions when you came in."

"Makes total sense," I said. "When they saw you with that camera, it looked to those kids as if you had just one huge eye. Probably you were smiling and your braces were flashing in the sunlight. You ran toward them, and they were convinced that you were an Evia. So they shouted a word you heard as 'evil' and ran into the woods to hide."

"There's a lesson here," Daniel said. "We should have told all of you not to take any photos without first asking the Achuar for permission to do so. My fault. Please don't take any more unless they give us permission."

Jessica would later tell me that the experience had given her a new awareness about how the presence of outsiders can affect a community and about the need to try to understand this before entering such a community. It was an important lesson in cultural sensitivity and an example, in my view, of the type of entitlement we Americans take for granted.

By the time we entered the community, the Achuar adults had convinced their children to come out of hiding. Most of the men knew Daniel and had helped in the construction of the lodge. The women were warier; however, after a half hour of conversation between our Achuar guide, Daniel, and the men, the women brought us chicha and, as is their custom, served each of us individually.

Daniel explained that chicha was not just a drink to the Achuar but also the thing they shared when communities came together. Serving it to us was a sign of friendship and trust.

Jessica demonstrated her camera to the children and tried to explain through sign language how it worked. Then the children invited her to join them as they kicked a small ball Daniel had given them around the clearing in the center of the community. The sounds of children giggling, shouting, and laughing were a reminder of our shared humanity.

As we prepared to head back to Kapawi, a group of Achuar women stood before us and sang several of their beautifully haunting songs. The sharing of chicha, the openness of the Achuar children after their initial fears, and now the songs of the women seemed a sign that there had been a breakthrough in communications between two groups from very diverse backgrounds in a short period of time. It seemed a good omen for developing a partnership with the Achuar and perhaps an indication of hope for the world as well.

That evening, back in the lodge, I explained that the Legend of the Evias, like all their mythologies and oral histories, is told by Shuar and Achuar elders to the children at night as people are preparing for bed and also early in the morning when they organize themselves for the day ahead.

"This legend is a teaching tool," I added, "that offers to help children learn about life. When you hear it, think about the message it sends to children. It instructs them to confront their fears. It says that they must do that alone. When they do, they gain confidence and strength. And that gives them the power to overcome their fears and move forward."

I repeated the legend as I had heard it told by a Shuar elder.

22

A SHAMAN'S STORY

A story told through the words of Chumbi, a Shuar elder and shaman:

The Evias were giant white cannibals who lived deep in the forest. We, the people, never went near where they lived. For as long as anyone could remember, they had stuck to themselves, never bothering us. And we were a happy, peaceful people.

Then one night they came into our community. They grabbed our women and children and ate them right in front of our men. Of course, the men picked up their spears and fought valiantly. But each time they stabbed one of the Evias, their weapons broke. There was nothing they could do. Then the Evias killed and ate our men. The only thing left for our people was to run into the forest and hide.

This began to happened frequently. Besides killing us, the huge Evias trampled the land, cut our trees for firewood, and used our rivers as toilets. We were terrified and defenseless.

One day a canoe came down the river carrying three warriors. The leader was large and heavily muscled. He seemed to shine with a special energy. His name was Etsaa and he said he'd come to save us from the Evias.

We were mystified. How would this man succeed where all our warriors had failed?

The next day, Etsaa disappeared into the forest. He left his men behind, saying "I have to do this alone. I can't take my men with me." We all knew that he would never return.

Days passed and there was no sign of Etsaa. Every morning we awoke expecting to be attacked by the Evias.

And then, miracle of all miracles, Etsaa emerged from the forest.

"I watched the Evias very carefully," he said. "I have a plan." He looked around at all of us. "But you must make some sacrifices."

"We will do anything," our people agreed.

"The Evias said that if your women provide them with lots of chicha and fruits, vegetables, and nuts, and your men give them the finest meats from the tapirs, boars, birds, and monkeys they hunt, they will spare your lives."

We knew that we and our children would go hungry. But we saw no alternative. We agreed.

It worked. The Evias kept their word. They stopped attacking us.

However, over time, our people began to suffer—horribly. There was simply not enough food for the Evias and us. We were starving.

"I can show you how to get rid of the Evias once and for all," Etsaa said. "But you must do something in return."

"Yes, of course," we said. "Whatever you want."

He asked if we had noticed that our populations had grown very large before the Evias arrived and that the animals and birds were becoming scarce and the forest smaller and smaller.

We talked among ourselves and saw that it was true.

"To the animals, the birds, the plants, and the trees, you are the cannibals," Etsaa said. "You are to them what the Evias are to you."

We had to admit that he was right.

"You have to change; you need to practice forms of birth control that I will teach you. You must keep your populations small and take care of all life around you. If you fail to do this, then you must do with yourselves what your women do with your gardens. You must weed your populations, even as the women weed the manioc groves."

We asked him what he meant by that.

"If you don't keep your populations in balance, you must go to war with each other, one clan against another."

It seemed like a simple request and we were certain that we could practice birth control and not have to kill each other. We agreed to his request.

"Good." He showed us how to poison the chicha and food we gave to the Evias and how to lay traps for them. "You can never kill them with your weapons, so you must use stealth, cunning, and tricks."

The tricks he taught us worked. Before long we had rid ourselves of the Evias. After that, Etsaa left. He rose up into the sky and became the sun. To this day we call the sun "Etsaa."

However, over time, we failed to keep our populations in check and that is why we were forced to go to war with other clans.

For the Achuar this legend was a lesson in self-discovery, as well as a good story. After reciting it, Chumbi always looked around at those who had been listening, which usually was mostly Shuar children. "You must ask yourself," he would say, "about the Evias in your life. What scares you? What are you doing to hurt the plants and animals, and other people? What must you do to change this? Realize that each of you has your own Evias. Each of you is Etsaa. Know that sometimes you must dive deep inside your heart to confront your Evias. You must do this alone. No one can help you. Only by doing that will you avoid going to war with yourself."

23

THE PAYOFF

THE NEXT MORNING OUR GROUP gathered for breakfast. There was talk about the destruction that the industrialized world was causing, that—like the Evias—we and our corporations were trampling the earth, cutting forests, polluting rivers, and gluttonously devouring everything in sight. Someone pointed out that if we continued on this path, at some point wars, disease epidemics, or some other acts of man or nature would have to weed out our populations. This Indigenous legend was seen as a message about the growing global crises.

Several people wanted to know what I'd meant when I'd mentioned that some of the Achuar and Shuar believe that we in the modern world and our oil companies are a current manifestation of the Evias.

"Missionaries don't value the Indigenous people's stories," I answered. "Etsaa is sacrilege to them. A few of the older Shuar men have told me of a time when they and the women practiced forms of birth control similar to Tantric practices and that the women also used certain plants to prevent pregnancy or cause abortions. Then the missionaries arrived. The Church forbids all birth control—except abstinence. And that is something the Achuar and Shuar are not about to practice. Also, both the missionaries and the government condemn warfare. We think of that as good, but it's also had a negative impact. Populations have mushroomed. The animals—the main source of protein in a jungle environment—are disappearing. Indigenous men and women throughout the Amazon are having to prostitute themselves to oil and construction companies just to feed their families. Some say that Etsaa is angry because they haven't kept their commitment. So, the Evias have returned."

"Compared to the Achuar, we're giants," someone observed. "White ones."

"Oil derricks, bulldozers, and other gigantic machines cannibalize the land," another added.

It was one more perception-changing moment for our group. Most of them had been educated to think of our culture as respected in places like the Amazon. Now, as we finished breakfast, there was a great deal of conversation around the idea that we were seen as giant white cannibals who came to exploit the Achuar and their neighbors.

After breakfast, we took the canoe ride to the home of Taish, the shaman Daniel, Ehud, Juan Gabriel, and I had visited before, where we'd taken ayahuasca and I'd gone on that shamanic journey through history. Daniel had assured me that there had been a peace treaty between Taish and the community that had attacked him. There was nothing to fear.

Taish welcomed Daniel, Juan Gabriel, and me with open arms and, through a young interpreter, greeted everyone. Although several of our people later remarked that he had the look of a fierce warrior, to me his appearance and attitude were gentler than a year earlier.

Shortly after we'd set up our mosquito-net tents beneath the palm-frond roof of his large home, the sun set. We gathered around Taish, sitting on wooden stools in a circle. He welcomed us once again and offered ayahuasca. This was a time when ayahuasca was still virtually unknown outside the Amazon. Only Lynne, Bill, and one other member decided to drink it, although several of those who declined asked for and received healings from Taish. Even for those who did not partake, it was a powerful night.

The shaman's melodious chanting, the sounds of the jungle, the scent of wood smoke mixed with night-blooming flowers, and what Daniel referred to as "the spirit of the plant" opened us all to the magic of this place. The tension and anxiety that had built inside me ever since Lynne and I had first started planning this trip melted into the night. For the first time, I felt a sense of relief.

The next morning, Daniel, Juan Gabriel, and I met with Taish and three Achuar warriors in the shaman's lodge. On that previous trip, Daniel had brought a gift of supplies to Taish; we had paid no money for the visit or the ayahuasca. This time, Daniel explained, we wanted to pay him in currency and also wanted to set a precedent for future visits of people who would be coming once the Kapawi Lodge was finished. He asked how much each of the three people who had drunk ayahuasca owed.

Taish conferred with his companions. "A thousand dollars," he said at last.

I was stunned. I looked from Daniel to Juan Gabriel. "I can't possibly ask our people to pay such an exorbitant price."

"We should have negotiated the price before the ceremony," Juan Gabriel said. It reminded me once again of the cultural biases even people who are sensitive to such things hold.

The three of us had a long conversation with Taish. He turned to the warriors. They gave us looks that made my blood run cold. One picked up his spear and jabbed it into the earthen floor of the lodge. Taish glared at us. "A thousand dollars," he repeated.

I recalled Daniel's comment months before: "You're going to have to agree to their request. They own the canoes." I also recalled the "kidnapping" in that other community. It seemed our whole group was now held hostage. What choice did we have but to capitulate? This surely would kill any chances for partnership.

We gathered the group. We sat in a circle on wooden stools. When we explained, their faces reflected the shock, anger, and fear that I felt.

"Must be a mistake," someone finally muttered.

Daniel jumped to his feet. "That's it!" He motioned to Juan Gabriel and me. "Come. Let's meet again with the shaman."

Without another word, Daniel turned and led us quickly to Taish, who had remained seated in his lodge. Unlike earlier, a long spear rested on his lap. More men were gathered around him.

The three of us sat down on a bench that faced the shaman.

Daniel asked me for ten dollars.

My hand shook as I took a ten dollar bill from my pocket and gave it to him.

He reached into his backpack, pulled a wad of bills out, counted them, and then handed the stack, along with my bill, to Taish. "Which do you want?" he asked.

Taish counted the bills in the stack and broke into a big grin. He waved them in the air. "This is it," he said. "This much from each of the three people who took the ayahuasca."

Daniel turned to Juan Gabriel and me. "He's thinking of sucres," he said, referring to the Ecuadorian currency. He grinned. "He's not asking for $1,000. He's asking for sucres that are worth less than five dollars."

The three of us began to laugh.

Taish looked puzzled, aggravated. He asked what we found so funny.

Daniel explained.

Taish slapped his knee. He and his men broke into fits of laughter. We all spent the next moments doubled over with the laughter that comes from the release of tension.

"Those sucres are not enough," Daniel said after we had collected ourselves. "You have shared with us your home, as well as your ayahuasca. We want to pay you more. We want to set a good precedent."

Taish thought about this and then quietly conferred in Achuar with the other men. "We trust you," he said at last. "Pay what is fair."

I wanted to hug him; instead I just said the Achuar words for *thank you*: "Makate."

We went back to our people. They were busily folding and packing the mosquito-net tents and their backpacks. It was obvious that they were struggling to take their minds off the negotiations. As soon as they saw us, they stopped and gathered around.

"It was all about perception," I said. "And cultural misunderstandings."

Daniel explained.

Tension-releasing laughter filled Taish's home.

In the end, we settled on a price that was equivalent to the amount a massage therapist would have charged in the US. It was a lot by Achuar standards and yet we all agreed that we needed to pay at least that much; we wanted to encourage them to view us as generous and also to understand that, despite what they'd heard from the missionaries, many in our community placed great value on the work of the shamans.

Departing from Taish's home, one by one our people expressed their gratitude for the magic they had experienced and for his hospitality. He, the warriors around him, and the entire family were beaming. We would all have stories to tell our grandchildren.

A potentially disastrous situation had shapeshifted into a bonding experience. And a foreign group of men, women, and a pre-teenage girl had spent a night in an Achuar shaman's home, an historical first.

"Mind-sets," Lynne reminded me as we walked into the forest. "In this case, perceptions about money. With Roberto Poz, it was his perception about our intent and his belief that Americans were untrustworthy. When he saw the sacred items from Ecuador, his perception of us and our motivations changed. Something along similar lines happened here."

An additional lesson, it seemed to me, was to avoid assumptions about the values and mind-sets of other people and cultures.

PART 7

CREATING A LIFE ECONOMY

1993–2017

The Life Economy cleans up pollution,
regenerates devastated environments,
recycles, and develops new technologies
that benefit people and nature. Businesses
that pay returns to investors who invest
in an economy that is itself a renewable
resource become the success stories.

24

COMING TOGETHER

DESPITE ALL MY YEARS with the Shuar and my previous trip to the Achuar, this visit with Taish and his people had offered new and powerful insights. Experiencing the ways individuals from my culture were impacted by people who were considered "primitive" by most of the world highlighted the important role that biases play in molding the realities of everyday life.

During our relatively brief time in the rain forest, five days and four nights, our group saw that the Achuar's relationship with money, the way they live as integral parts of the natural world, their long-term commitments to future generations, and a spirituality that revolves around the personal interconnectedness they have with plants, animals, the rivers, and the earth instills in them a very different worldview from that offered by cultures like ours. Whereas our education taught us to objectify nature and to view it as separate from us, and our religions elevated humans to special positions, theirs taught that people are just one thread in the rich fabric of the universe.

The experiences there impacted everyone in our group. They strengthened my resolve to facilitate the realization of the prophecy that the Eagles and the Condors will join together to create a new consciousness about what it means to be members of the most dominant species on this planet. Those experiences had a profound impact on Lynne; she would later write in her book, *The Soul of Money*,

> It was there in Achuar territory that we had an encounter with the leaders of the Achuar people that has completely changed my life. Here in this

rain forest, abundant and overflowing with beauty and life, were people who wore the face paint and yellow-and-red feather crowns I recognized from my dream. They looked like they had come from another age, but they were as sophisticated in their ways and as evolved as the most evolved of all of us.[1]

That sophistication showed up continually during those five days and four nights. We learned through conversations with many Achuar that they understood that the problems they confront in their corner of the world are symbolic of what they believe will happen everywhere, unless we humans change. They had invited us to their lands and into their homes to save their forests and also because they wanted to partner with us to help humans everywhere understand the need to transform our relationship with the natural world. They emphasized that the survival of their forests is tied to the survival of all global systems. The future of the world, they said, depends on a change in human attitudes, and such a change, in turn, depends on a new dream for humanity—of what it means to be humans living on this fragile space station called Earth.

There was a shared feeling among our group of amazement that people who had only recently been in contact with the outside world had such deep wisdom and knowledge. Most of our members had assumed that the outside world, their world, our world, had all the answers; when they left, that belief had been upended.

"It's truly as though the forest is speaking to the Achuar and they are conveying the message to us," Lynne said during an evening meeting.

The Achuar's request to us was twofold. Their first ask was that we help them face their fears and learn the ways of modern cultures so they can prepare to deal with those cultures and with the growing threats from oil companies. Their second ask was that we face our own fears, let go of a belief system that separates us from everything nonhuman, learn about the importance of living in harmony with nature, protect future generations of all species, and spread a message that convinces people around the world to do the same.

"Our visions show that you who have come here are the opposite of the Evias," one elder told us. "You are like Etsaa in modern form. You've arrived to teach us to defend ourselves against the Evias. They come from your lands, but you are not the same as them."

All the members of our group were deeply touched by the message and by the passion and eloquence of the people who delivered it. Beyond that, they also saw the practical side. These Achuar were storytellers with a rich oral tradition who expressed themselves beautifully, and they also were hunters and gatherers who were deeply connected to the earth and who understood the importance of working together as integrated parts of a greater whole, in a manner that benefits the entire community.

This practical side had created an organization in 1991 called OINAE (Organización Interprovincial de la Nacionalidad Achuar del Ecuador). Although it was similar to Shuar and Kichwa federations that enjoyed legal status under Ecuadorian law, it had not yet satisfied all the government's requirements. The Achuar were working on making that happen.

Part of that process required that the newly elected officials of OINAE set up an office in Puyo, a town near the Shell airstrip that was a meeting place for people from all over the Ecuadorian Amazon. That office, we were told, was poorly furnished. The Achuar needed to find ways to buy equipment, pay the rent, and provide a room and food for the three leaders who managed it.

On the day we flew out of Achuar Territory, our bus met us in Shell and drove us to Puyo. A combination of jungle runners, shortwave radios, and bush pilots had delivered word of our arrival. The three Achuar leaders greeted us at the door to their office, but neither they nor their office were at all what we'd expected.

25

COMMITMENT

THE THREE MEN IN PUYO looked more like business executives than the Achuar we were accustomed to seeing. Gone were the painted faces, traditional ankle-length kilts, and feathered crowns. Instead, they were dressed in starched and collared white shirts, pressed slacks, and formal black shoes.

They shook our hands and invited us into a dilapidated wooden shack. As we squeezed ourselves into the crammed space, the contrast between this office and their homes in the jungle could not have been greater. The stale air in the windowless room reeked of mold. The meager furnishings consisted of a wobbly desk, four rickety wooden chairs, and a battered vintage typewriter.

After apologizing for the lack of chairs, one of the men proudly pointed at the typewriter. "Our first big purchase," he said. "We're hoping for a telephone next."

"But unfortunately," a second added, "even if we could afford the phone, we'd have to pay a fortune to have the lines come here." He shook his head sadly. "For now," he pointed through the open doorway where several in our group were standing, "we have to go to the store down that road and pay to use theirs."

Daniel, who had been interpreting, told them that we felt honored to meet with them in their office. He summarized our experiences in Kapawi and explained that we had come to offer our support.

After the first man spoke again, Daniel explained, "He's the president of this new Achuar organization. He wants you to know that they've heard about the help Dream Change has given to the Shuar and about the intent of this group to support the Achuar. He thanks you for that. He repeated much of what's been said these past days about the importance of living in harmony with nature. He's very grateful that you're here and committed to helping the Achuar and to changing the dream of your people. He and the other two leaders are prepared to answer any questions you may have." Daniel looked around. "Questions?"

"How do you like living in Puyo, instead of the rain forest?" a woman asked.

The three exchanged glances. "We miss our families," one replied.

"And the forests," another added. "But we must do this if we are to survive as a people, a culture—a nation."

Over the ensuing couple of hours, they presented us with a detailed plan of exactly what they needed to accomplish in the next few weeks and months and for years ahead. They had developed lists, charts, and hand-drawn maps of their territory.

My heart felt as if it would burst with emotion as I heard these men and watched the faces of our group. It seemed both wonderful and unbelievable that the Achuar—the people in the jungle who had welcomed us into their families and now these men who had developed this sophisticated plan—were the same people that Captain Espinoza had feared as "killers" back in my Peace Corps days. And that they represented the men who less than two years before had attacked the plane I shared with Yahanua and had also tried to assassinate Taish. It seemed that something almost beyond imagining had happened, something magical. In a very brief time the Achuar had learned to deal with each other and with cultures that were so different from their own—ours and those of neighbors who had been their enemies—and now were determined to build alliances to protect their lands, their cultural values, and the entire world. I was astounded that all this could happen at all; yet, here it was barely more than two decades since I'd come to these lands as a Peace Corps volunteer. I asked myself, If they can do that, can't we all make the changes that will allow our species to survive and thrive in a sustainable world?

By the time we said our goodbyes, it was evident that a group of people who had never been in this rain forest before, who had come with misgivings and trepidation, was completely captivated. Walking away from that humble office, a wave of gratitude and well-being swept through me. It seemed that, despite all the drama and the potential pitfalls, the partnership the Achuar had requested during those long nights in the meeting lodge a couple of years earlier might have begun to materialize.

Our bus headed back up the Pastaza River gorge, taking us toward our first post-jungle night. In the town of Baños, hot showers, flush toilets, and a western-style hotel awaited us, as well as dinner at a local Italian restaurant. I could see that, as much as they'd enjoyed their adventure in the rain forest, these people were grateful to be returning to a world that was more familiar to them—another sign that old patterns of comfort and privilege are hard to break.

I sat with Jessica in the front of the bus. At one point, I stood up and looked around at our companions. They were dirty, muddy, exhausted, and yet—they were all talking excitedly and laughing.

"You're glowing," Jessica said. "A few days with the Achuar and it looks like these people are ready to make something happen."

I shared with her my dream that out of this gathering would come a working and lasting partnership with the Achuar. I had no idea that we had planted a seed that eventually would take root and reach around the planet.

The dream took another step toward becoming a reality during breakfast the next morning, our final day together before driving to Quito, separating, and flying to our respective homes. Dave Ellis, an author of books and a creator of inspirational, motivational programs, launched a fundraising appeal. By the time we had polished off the last pot of coffee and were about to board our bus, the group had committed $120,000 to, in Dave's words, "forge a partnership that will save the rain forests and change the dream of the modern world."

Then suddenly, unexpectedly, I was struck by another feeling, an anxiousness that lodged in the pit of my gut. It seemed odd when I felt it as I stepped aboard the bus. It seemed even odder that it grew heavier as we traveled from Baños toward Quito. Why? What was happening to me?

Jessica gave me a quizzical look. "What's going on, Dad? You seem uptight."

"I'm not sure." Her question forced me to put a name to my feelings. "A little depressed, I guess. Worried."

"About . . . ?"

I thought for a moment. "Well, everyone got excited. They've offered all this money." I paused and forced myself to think. Then it came to me. "But who's going to make the partnership happen? I'm already overwhelmed with Dream Change and the Shuar. All the people on this bus will just return to their normal lives. I'm stuck with the outcome. Where do we go from here?"

Jessica gave me a sympathetic look. Then her face brightened. "Ask them." She pointed toward the back of the bus. "Someone will have the answer."

I stared at her. It was hard to believe that she was only twelve years old. Her optimism was infectious. "OK. Thanks." I stood up and asked the driver to turn on the microphone. "Hi, guys," I said, trying to draw them out of their conversations. "Wow, what a trip! What a group of people!"

They broke into cheers.

"Are you feeling inspired?"

More cheers.

"Me too. But . . ." My gaze traveled from one to another. "I'm also worried. We've made promises to the Achuar. You committed to donating money and to forming a partnership and developing a plan to help them complete the things they outlined. That's absolutely wonderful." I paused. "But, as I've said before, I'm already overextended in my work with the Shuar." I made eye contact with each of them. "Who will collect the money, take responsibility for setting up a partnership, and move this forward?"

There was dead silence.

I glanced around again, taking in each and every one of them. They looked at someone else, out the window, anywhere but at me. I peered down at Jessica. She smiled sweetly and gave me a thumbs up. The silence seemed eternal.

Finally, Bill Twist's eyes met mine. He stood up and took the microphone. "I'll do it," he said. "But just for the first three months."

Three months turned into a lifetime. As a result of that trip, Bill ended up quitting his job as CEO of a highly successful financial services company. He, Lynne, a group of friends, and I created a 501(c)(3) nonprofit organization, the Pachamama Alliance—named for the Quichua word that means "Mother Earth, Mother Universe, Mother of All Space and Time." Bill became the organization's chairman of the board and then its executive director. During the years to come, he would oversee the staffing of offices in San Francisco and Quito and a network of volunteers in more than eighty countries. Lynne would take charge of raising funds to finance the many projects that support the Achuar and other Indigenous nations and that develop inspirational programs aimed at changing the destructive dream of the modern world in countries on every continent.

From the beginning, the Pachamama Alliance's programs have been deeply influenced by the rain forest people's philosophy that objective reality is molded by perceptions. For them, the "dream" is not limited to what happens while we're sleeping; it includes the way our lives are determined by our mind-sets and the impacts those have on our values, intentions, and actions. The Pachamama Alliance programs focus on transforming a culture of separation and overconsumption into one that honors and sustains life and, in the language of the Pachamama Alliance's mission statement, "empowers indigenous people of the Amazon rainforest to preserve their lands and culture and, using insights gained from that work, to educate and inspire individuals everywhere to bring forth a thriving, just and sustainable world." This work includes training facilitators who take groups into Achuar Territory—and to many other Indigenous communities—where they learn about facilitating personal and global transformation.

It would later become apparent that all of us—people from the Amazon and the industrialized world—were coming together to create a social-governmental-economic system that will serve the future of life on our planet. The result is a Life Economy. The Life Economy cleans up pollution, regenerates devastated environments, recycles, and develops new technologies that benefit people and nature. Businesses that pay returns to investors who invest in an economy that is itself a renewable resource become the success stories.

When I asked Bill many years later what had motivated him to take the microphone on that bus, he told me that, because of his background in business and finance, he figured the tasks involved would be relatively easy for him. "Besides," he said, "no one else was stepping to the plate and it was important to keep the momentum moving forward." He paused, smiled. "In truth, if someone else had offered, I would have been disappointed. I'd had a very powerful experience with the Achuar. I'd been deeply taken by the beauty and abundance of their territory. I had been struck by the grounded strength and stoic presence of the Achuar men and, in particular, the powerful warrior and skilled hunter who, as our guide, shared his knowledge of the forest with us. Walter [the name given to him by missionaries] was aware of everything and was able to anticipate the needs and idiosyncrasies of everyone in our group. I was fascinated to imagine the world as it appeared to him. How was he able to be so appropriate with us, people so different? What did he see and know that allowed him to be so present? Taking on the role of organizing things for the group made it easy for me to stay involved in a way that would probably lead me to come back to Ecuador—something I very much wanted to do."

Equally significant to what transpired at the Pachamama Alliance is the way the Achuar, Shuar, Sapara, Kichwa, Shiwiar, and other Indigenous people of Ecuador changed their relationships to each other. Longtime enemies joined forces. They put aside their fears, touched a huge and fierce jaguar that had held them back for centuries, and joined forces. By example, they became the poster children for many people around the world seeking positive change through new thinking and actions that serve the needs of their communities, all humankind, and the natural world.

The Achuar continued to work on gaining the same legal status as the Shuar and Kichwa federations and within four years of our visit, they succeeded; the name was eventually shortened from OINAE to NAE (Nacionalidad Achuar del Ecuador).

NAE joined a coalition that includes many Amazonian Indigenous nations, known as CONFENIAE (Confederación de Nacionalidades Indígenas de la Amazonía Ecuatoriana). It is one of the three legs that compose CONAIE (Confederación de Nacionalidades Indígenas del Ecuador), a powerful alliance that represents Indigenous nations from the three regions (the Amazon, Andes, and Coast). These federations have been extremely successful at influencing Ecuador's national and international policies, and they now serve as models for Indigenous organizations across the planet. The Pachamama Alliance has supported them and their movements by donating money, equipment, and supplies and by providing legal and business advice.

Although from the beginning I've served on the Pachamama Alliance board, from the late 1990s until 2001, I continued to focus most of my efforts on Dream Change and the Shuar. My life changed when I was rushed, dying, to a New York City hospital . . .

26

POISONED

BY 2001 MY CONTRACT with SWEC had ended and I was thinking a lot about that book I'd stopped writing back when I received those threatening phone calls. I just couldn't get it out of my mind.

On September 11, 2001, I was leading a Dream Change group to the Shuar, deep in the Amazon. When the World Trade towers were attacked, I happened to be on a shortwave radio with the pilot up in the Andes who was scheduled to pick us up several days later. He was listening to a commercial radio station and described minute by minute the seemingly impossible events in New York. That night, a Shuar shaman offered our group a ceremony that helped us deal with the shock and fear we all were experiencing.

When I returned to the United States, I flew to New York City. Looking down into that horrible pit, I knew that it was time to write about what had been on my mind, the things I'd done as an economic hit man. While I didn't see a direct connection with 9/11, I felt it imperative that I disclose a few of the reasons some people in other countries resent the US. Since my obligations to SWEC were over, I was under no legal restrictions. My only hesitation was the fear that my family and I might once again be threatened by assassins. So this time I decided to make it a personal story, a confession, and not to contact any other people who had been involved in my line of work or that of the jackals. I would write the entire manuscript in secret and then send it to my agent, Paul Fedorko, in New York. I figured that once it was in his very capable hands and he had sent it to publishers, it was my best insurance policy. Anyone who might want to kill me would know that making me a martyr would sell lots of books.

Confessions was rejected by thirty-nine publishers—mostly because they feared the repercussions. Paul kept trying and also was a master at soothing my ego. Finally, a California house, Berrett-Koehler, had the courage to publish it in late 2004. It quickly went to the *New York Times* nonfiction bestseller list and has been there for more than seventy weeks.

Five months after the book was published, in March of 2005, I flew again to New York City, where I was scheduled to speak at the United Nations. I was doing a lot of media interviews in those days. My publicist, Peg Booth, had phoned a few days before the New York trip to tell me that a man who identified himself as a freelance journalist had requested an interview. Since he was not associated with any particular paper or magazine, I at first declined. I was prioritizing my meetings—which often included meals—with reporters from known news outlets.

The journalist persisted. "He offered to meet you at the airport, or drive you to a couple of venues, and take you to a meal," Peg told me on a follow-up call. "He'll drop you off at the friend's apartment where you're staying." We agreed that this sounded a lot better than taking taxis.

He and I chatted about my upcoming UN talk as we drove to a small Italian café on the Upper East Side. I was not in the least bit concerned. I was convinced that killing me would publicize my story, and that was the last thing the CIA or anyone else who might hire jackals would want. We ordered our food, and I got up and went to the men's room before the spaghetti bolognese arrived. When I returned, the food was on the table. While we ate, he asked a few questions that were so simple I wondered how he ever managed to sell his articles. We had a nice meal, he dropped me off, and that, I thought, was the end of our connection.

After leaving him, I was alone in my friend's apartment getting ready to meet with my literary agent, Paul, when, without warning, I was overcome with severe cramps. I stumbled to the bathroom; sitting on the toilet, blood poured out of me. By the time Paul arrived, I was lying on the floor, shaking violently, in shock. Rushed to Lenox Hill Hospital, I was told that I had lost more than half the blood in my body and was immediately given transfusions. Later, surgeons operated on me for six hours; they removed more than seventy percent of my colon.

As I lay recovering in that hospital bed, I received emails and phone calls from reporters, Pachamama Alliance people, and many friends, including people who were certain that I'd been poisoned. The more I've thought about it, the more convinced I've become that the facts supported this conclusion. I'd undergone a standard "after-fifty" precautionary colonoscopy a few months earlier, and my Florida gastroenterologist had told me that, other than having some diverticula like most people my age, my colon was in good shape. I'd experienced no symptoms, no previous pain or bleeding. As a martial artist, two days before flying to New York, I'd worked out strenuously with other black belts and been in great shape. As I thought back, I realized that my visit to the restroom during the meal had given the "freelance journalist" plenty of time to poison my food.

The New York doctors had been preoccupied with keeping me alive. No one had considered the possibility that I'd been poisoned until after the operation—and the only evidence had been incinerated. Although I'd been threatened in the past by anonymous phone calls and a man claiming to represent Ecuadorian oil interests and hassled by US customs officials, I'd figured that the book's publication protected me. Now, that assumption seemed a mistake. Attempts to contact the "freelance journalist" failed. In any case, we had no evidence for charging him with a possible crime.

During those first days after my operation, my emotions bounced from relief that I was alive to fear that there would be another attempt to murder me—or do something terrible to Jessica and Winifred, who had flown to New York to be at my bedside. I warned them to be vigilant.

Then a phone call with an old friend who had been a mercenary jackal working for government intelligence agencies in Africa, the Middle East, and the US suggested something else.

"That guy sounds too stupid and unprofessional to be a CIA or an NSA asset," he said. "If he worked for one of the alphabet agencies, you'd be dead."

"Who then?"

"My guess? A fanatic. Someone who hates you for what you did as an economic hit man." He paused. "Or because you came clean and wrote about it."

I felt a rush of relief. Then another horrible thought stopped me. "Do you think he'll try again?"

There was silence for a moment. "I doubt it," he finally replied. "Nuts like that are usually erratic people. If they fail, they're likely to think it isn't worth the risk of a second shot. In this case, the dude's reading all the internet chatter about you. He knows you've suffered a lot, lost most of your colon, and missed a UN speech and dozens of other venues and that you are probably scared out of your wits and will be very careful in the future." He chuckled. "He's basking in his weird world of glory."

After he hung up, I felt like a man reprieved. I lay in bed, alone in that hospital room, and allowed the sense of liberation to take me into a deep sleep.

However, as soon as I woke up, I was aware of another disturbing question. Maybe it had come through a dream. How many other people hate me, I wondered, for what I did as an EHM or for trying to right those wrongs?

Surrounded by those gray hospital walls, the scream of sirens outside my window, the moans of the sick and dying inside, the endless call for doctors over the PA system, the odor of antiseptic, and all the other sights, sounds, and smells that attack the senses in a hospital—especially one located in a very old and musty New York City building—I tumbled into the dark abyss of self-recrimination.

One night, a nurse shook me awake. "You were screaming," she murmured. "Are you in pain?"

I lay there, looking up at her face, haunted by the memory of a dream. A ferocious jaguar had threatened to attack me. Two questions rang in my ears: Why did you stay at that evil job so long? Couldn't you see that you were colonizing vulnerable people?

"Are you in pain?" she persisted.

"Just a nightmare," I finally managed.

She patted my shoulder. "You've been through a traumatic operation."

For days, as I continued to recover, I kept hearing those same questions. Why had I stayed in that job all those years, even after I'd come to realize that what I was doing was wrong? What had kept me from seeing that our form of colonization was hurting us, the colonizers, as well as the colonized? The failed global economic system we created and our obsession with short-term profit maximization, regardless of the environmental and social costs, had resulted in terrible environmental devastation, income inequality, wars, and social and political collapse in many countries. The only answer I could come up with was that it had been excruciatingly difficult to escape from MAIN. I'd been seduced by the money, flying first class, staying in the best hotels, and all the other perks. I'd also yielded to the pressure exerted by my boss, other executives, and my fellow employees. They'd offered every sort of carrot and stick to convince me to stay.

But there'd been more to it. The aura of the job itself had kept me there. I was accomplishing what I'd been schooled to accomplish. I was making money and traveling to places I'd never imagined I'd ever visit. I was meeting presidents. I was living the privileged life that I'd been taught was the American dream. I was an economist doing what economists in international development work are supposed to do. I was chief economist. The title was a sort of egotistical placard glued to my name, the identity I presented to the world and to the face that I shaved in my mirror. Beyond that, I was an American. I had a responsibility to sell American capitalism to all those people in countries that were tempted to embrace the Soviets and communism.

Not long after I was released from Lenox Hill Hospital, I traveled to Boston, where I reconnected with Howard Zinn, my former Boston University professor and the author of many books, including the bestseller *A People's History of the United States*. Then in his eighties, Howard devoted himself to continuing what he'd done all his professional life, campaigning to reform a system that was failing. When I shared with him my feelings of guilt, his response reminded me of the Indigenous advice I'd received.

"Don't run from the guilt," Howard said. "We're all guilty. We have to admit that although the big corporations own the propaganda machines, we allow ourselves to be duped. You can set an example. Show people that the way out, redemption, comes from confronting and changing it. Roll up your sleeves, take action."

Howard was urging me to see that I'd succumbed to an idea of success that had been ingrained in me by many years of education and socialization.

That perception had sent me into a reality that no longer served me. I remembered the shamans I'd known. Changing it was quite simple. All it required was recognizing those ingrained ideas, those perceptions, touching and changing them, and then acting to create a new reality. Unfortunately, I wasn't quite ready to do that.

27

BREAKING OLD IDEAS

FOR THE FOUR YEARS following the publication of *Confessions*, I was inundated with requests to give speeches and media interviews in many foreign countries, as well as throughout the US. During the times I was home, I spent hours in interviews by phone or through the internet.

Because of the book's success and the prospect of large profits, the major houses that had originally rejected it went into a bidding war to purchase the paperback rights. With my consent, Berrett-Koehler sold them to Penguin. After that, in addition to all the speaking and media venues, I also ended up with a contract from Penguin to write *The Secret History of the American Empire* and another from Random House to write *Hoodwinked*. I was too busy to think about much else. I now suspect that I was also running away from doing more, from following Howard's advice.

By 2009, things had slowed down and Howard's words began to haunt me: "Roll up your sleeves, take action." I realized that to act with integrity and effectiveness, I needed to rid myself of the perceptions that had built up during my life about my superiority as a white male born and educated in the United States. I had to drop my romantic views about the heroism of colonists on the American frontier who fought and ruthlessly killed native peoples through the use of superior weapons, treachery, lies, and broken treaties and imprisoned the survivors in concentration camp–like reservations. I had to bury all the anti–African American, anti-Vietnamese, anti-Chinese, anti-Muslim, anti-female, anti-gay, and all the other *antis* about people who did not look like me or did not embrace similar attitudes to mine. I had to reject a great deal of everything I'd learned in school, especially business school. I had to drop the colonizing concepts that portrayed the environment as needing to be either ravaged to exploit its oil, minerals, and lumber or protected because of the medicines, air, water, and other resources it offered to benefit humans. I had to expand my consciousness to accept the Indigenous idea that nature must be protected because she is alive and sacred. I had to admit that my ideas about myself and my role in business had helped create systems that are destroying life as we know it. I had to transform my fear into a commitment and actions to create a better world.

As a first step, I called Bill and Lynne and told them I'd like to get more deeply involved in the Pachamama Alliance. They embraced the idea enthusiastically. Beginning in 2010, I became a much more active board member.

The poisoning, the experience in the hospital, my meeting with Howard Zinn, and the insights I'd gained about my EHM job and the seductiveness of that sort of life transported me from an old reality to a new reality. It also helped me frame the idea of the jaguar we must touch. I saw that the jaguar stands on a Perception Bridge that can transport us between two realities.

28

THE PERCEPTION BRIDGE

WHEN ENTSÁ INTRODUCED ME to the idea of gaining wisdom, strength, and personal power from touching the jaguar, it made sense because of the healing, the transformation, I experienced. He had used the word for shapeshifting, "Arutam."

Now I came to understand the more philosophical concepts behind it. I recalled Maria Juana's words. I'd written them in my notebook: "There are two realities. Objective, like this chair, and perceived, the ideas discussed while sitting in this chair. By changing perceived reality, we transform objective reality." She had pointed out that if we perceive that only a certain kind of person, like a shaman, is allowed to sit in that chair, the chair and the conversations that happen around it take on a different reality than if we perceive the chair as available to everyone.

I also remembered Professor Mata telling me that the jaguar is a powerful symbol that, when I confronted it, faced my fears, would guide me to taking actions that would change my reality; in that case, make me healthy. And that did in fact become my new reality.

All my experiences over the years had enabled me to see clearly that human reality is molded by our perceptions; that this is the basis for modern psychotherapy, quantum physics, and corporate marketing; and that to change ourselves or our world, we must break through the barriers that imprison us in old ways of thinking and acting. If we run from, or deny, our fears, they will hound us. By confronting them, we take their power.

Now, I understood the jaguar's connection. It stood on a Perception Bridge that could convey us from a reality based on preconceived ideas and values to a reality based on new ideas and values. If we were scared off by that jaguar, held back by things we'd been taught in the past or our fear of change, for example, we could not get past the jaguar and cross the bridge. If, on the other hand, we touched the jaguar, recognized the voices, teachings, values, or other barriers that stood in our way, confronted them and altered them, we were empowered to take the actions necessary to cross the bridge into a new reality.

This could be understood in the context of the experience with Entsá all those many years before when I was dying in El Milagro. I began to form a mental image of two circles that represented the two realities and were connected by a bridge: Reality 1 leads across a Perception Bridge to create Reality 2.

In the case of my sickness and healing as a Peace Corps volunteer in the Amazon, Reality 1 was chicha (spit beer) and strange foods. The perception, a voice saying "This food and drink will kill you," transported me across a Perception Bridge to Reality 2: I was sick and dying.

The shamanic journey changed that perception. It started at the same Reality 1: chicha and strange foods. Then the new perception: images showing that the foods made the Shuar strong and the chicha purified the water. This offered to take me across the Perception Bridge to a new Reality 2: good health.

Guarding that Perception Bridge was a jaguar—at the beginning, that voice from the past saying that the food and drink were dangerous. When Entsá encouraged me to confront my fear, the jaguar empowered me to see that the food and drink were nourishing. It was my mind-set, my perception, that had held me back from ending my sickness, and now, by changing that perception, I became healthy.

I also realized that although I was diagnosed in Cuenca with parasites, these had likely been contracted from raw fruits, vegetables, and other foods I ate in "civilized" places like Cuenca or the cockroach-infested inn where we spent the night in transit to El Milagro, rather than the cooked foods in the jungle.

During the years following this revelation about the Perception Bridge, I worked on moving from one way of looking at my role as a human being living at this time in history to a new perception and a new reality. The actions I took and the ways I used my time changed and helped me envision a plan for transformation that was bigger than anything I could have imagined previously. I understood that when I touched the jaguar, I was able to see things from a different perspective. I was able to have compassion and empathy for the "other." For example, I found myself asking questions like, How does that CEO feel when he is attacked by environmentalists? What is needed to help him feel less threatened and more inspired to take the actions the environmentalists want him to take? How can we help him cross the Perception Bridge?

Furthermore, I came to see that my credentials as an economist gave me credibility among business leaders and the media and in academic circles. It was important that I stop chastising myself as a former EHM and instead focus on the experiences and knowledge I'd gained as a chief economist.

It also was a turning point for my family. Jessica had completed college, married, and had a son, Grant. Winifred and I concluded that our paths were leading in very different directions and decided to get divorced. As we went through the process, I was aware of old attitudes that created barriers to the type of divorce that would allow us to continue our friendship. There was, for example, one perception that assured me that I was being cheated financially and I should worry more about money than about my future with Winifred. When I became aware of these old attitudes, touched those jaguars, I received the gift of empathy for her and compassion for myself. I realized that our future relationship was more important than the relatively small amount of money in contention. Our decision to divorce freed us both in many ways. The manner in which we did it, with understanding and kindness toward each other, allowed us afterward to continue to be good friends and support each other on new levels.

I moved into a relationship with Kiman Lucas, the woman I now have lived with for many years. Both of us are high-strung, passionate, and emotional. When we have disagreements, if we see that the solution lies in a greater understanding of and more empathy for each other's feelings, we are taken across the Perception Bridge from what could have been an ugly reality to a much better, more beautiful one. Kiman, who is a lawyer, describes this process in a way that reflects her profession. "Reality 1," she says, "are the written laws. The way we perceive them, confront and change how others try to interpret them, has a huge impact on the outcome of a judicial case. Reality 2 is reflected by the outcome of the case. 'Guilty' or 'not guilty' is molded by the perceptions of judges or jurors."

It became apparent to me that we needed to touch the jaguar that is our fear of change, progressing from a destructive reality to one that brings us into harmony with nature and each other. This would be the only way to transform a failed global social-governmental-economic system to a successful one and to convince business leaders and all of us to embrace the values centered on long-term sustainability that our Indigenous allies were offering us.

29

THE ALLIANCE

BILL, LYNNE, AND I DECIDED THAT, along with Daniel, we would lead annual Founders Trips to the place where it had all begun. We included two amazing women: Belén Páez, who had run our Ecuadorian office from the beginning, and Sara Vetter, who had become Lynne's co-fundraiser. These women exemplify the practical aspects of altering reality by changing perceptions.

Belén was instrumental in forging a new constitution for Ecuador, the first in the world to guarantee the legal rights of nature. She also facilitated major changes in perceptions among Indigenous men and women around gender issues. Under her tutelage and that of her Shuar friend, Narcisa Mishienta, Indigenous women have become empowered to take leadership roles in community and national politics and governance.

Sara emphasizes that the value of money is determined by the ways we perceive it. She encourages people to understand that money is merely a means to an end and that one of the most important ends is the transition from failed systems to ones that will sustain life for future generations. She inspires people to employ money to create a Life Economy.

A call from the rain forest in 1993 and a pilgrimage by a dozen people into Achuar Territory in 1995 had evolved into a highly successful organization and an amazing partnership with Indigenous people. It was a great example of crossing the Perception Bridge. Changes in the way that first group perceived the world took them and many other people after them from one reality to another. For some, it required touching the jaguar of discouragement: "The problem is just too big." For some, the jaguar was a lack of confidence: "I'm not capable of solving this problem." For others, it was fear of change: "I don't want to risk losing the lifestyle I'm accustomed to." Whatever the jaguar they faced, once they understood and dealt with it, they became empowered to take actions that transported them into a new and empowering reality.

By 2020, the Pachamama Alliance was truly global, offering programs in more than eighty countries. At the beginning of its third decade, the Pachamama Alliance had a website, www.pachamama.org, that summarized its many accomplishments. Below are excerpts from that summary:

The Pachamama Alliance

Since 1997 we have worked in solidarity with Indigenous organizations of Ecuador's Amazon to defend their rights and homeland.

Our initial efforts provided legal and technical expertise to strengthen indigenous self-governance and preserve their lands and cultures . . .

While [these] were a profound success, we continued to inquire for many years into how to make a widespread impact to "change the dream."

In 2005, we launched our transformative learning workshops with the Awakening the Dreamer Symposium.

People gather at Symposiums around the world to discover the value of ancient wisdom in addressing our modern crises.[1]

Since 1997, enormous changes have occurred in the Ecuadorian Amazon. The road between Quito and Shell has been paved and widened. The new turboprop airplanes are equipped with state-of-the-art navigational technology. Many more people inhabit the areas along the road and have electricity and televisions. While these changes look good as development metrics, it is debatable whether they are truly beneficial or detrimental; they increase the possibilities for more exploitation, over-population, and the destruction of nature.

There is no question that positive changes have occurred. The oil companies have been stopped from expanding into Achuar Territory. Awareness about the importance of conserving the rain forests has increased—in

Ecuador and around the globe. Perhaps most incredible of all is the change that has transpired among the people themselves.

Some of the Achuar warriors who attacked our plane and tried to kill Yahanua are now married to Shuar women. The community that "kidnapped" Bill and Lynne's group on that third plane now works in close partnership with the Pachamama Alliance. Taish and his former enemies live together in peace. All the Amazonian nations, after centuries of animosity and warfare, have come together in federations with shared goals and values—and unified actions—that twenty years ago could not have been imagined.

And yet the news of the devastation we humans are causing our planet has grown increasingly dire.

By the time I sat down to write these words, it had become clear that the call from the forest was a call to gain new insights, adopt new values, and take the actions required to reprogram the navigational system of this space station where we live. It was a plea to save the world from the brutally destructive ways we have been treating ourselves and our home.

A visit to an Indigenous culture that knows a great deal about both colonization and decolonization helped bring all this together for me.

PART 8

DECOLONIZATION

2017–Present

We are the Elder Siblings—our culture
is older and wiser than yours. Our job is to
show you, the Younger Siblings, about
taking care of our sacred mother, the earth.
We resisted colonization, but the minds
of the Younger Siblings have been invaded
with the ideas of the colonizers.

30

THE KOGI
Experts in Colonization

IN THE FALL OF 1976, when I still worked for MAIN, I was riding a horse through lush jungles and up into the Sierra Nevada de Santa Marta mountains on the Caribbean coast of Colombia, the only place in the world where mainland mountains rise from the depths of the ocean to more than eighteen thousand feet. I was headed to a coffee farm I'd purchased as a personal project to work with a local university. I told myself that I wanted to show farmers how to grow their crops without chemicals. Looking back, I suspect it may have been a way of subconsciously trying to compensate for my EHM work and the privileges I enjoyed as a US citizen who in one week was paid a salary that was probably worth more than these subsistence farmers made in a lifetime. The farm consisted of about 250 acres of rugged mountainous rain forest. Roughly fifty of those acres had been planted in coffee trees. I'd never penetrated the dense jungle of the other two hundred acres.

A man on horseback was coming down the trail, leading two other horses. Each was carrying a load covered with a tarp. As they approached, I saw feet sticking out from under the tarps. Dead bodies! Two of them. Despite the heat, a cold shiver ran through me.

"What happened?" I asked the man as he pulled up beside me.

"They shot each other."

I was horrified. "Why? Who are they?"

"A drug trafficker and an FBI agent."

I stared at him. "That can't be. The FBI only works in the United States."

He reached into his saddlebag, pulled out something that I took for a wallet, and handed it to me. An FBI badge.

I was seized by a terrifying thought. What if some of the locals resented me as a foreign colonist, had planted marijuana and cocaine on my lands, and notified the FBI that I was a drug dealer?

I turned my horse around, headed down the trail in front of the man and his two corpses, got into the jeep I'd left parked at the side of the road below, and drove myself to the city of Barranquilla. I went immediately to the office of a Colombian friend who was in the coffee business and sold— practically gave—my farm to him.

Thirty-eight years later, I returned to the Sierra Nevada mountains. My friend and the person who had first introduced me to the Achuar, Daniel Koupermann, had visited the Kogi, who lived in those mountains. They had invited him and, through him, me to bring people to them. They'd told him that they had much to teach us about our role as earth stewards.

Daniel and I took groups to them in 2015 and 2016. Their message was always powerful, but with each trip they opened up more to us. Now, in 2017, the Kogi *Mamos* (male shamans) had invited our third group to a sacred site that until now, they said, had never been visited by outsiders.

We were sitting in a cave formed by mammoth stones, twelve visitors, two Mamos, and a young Mamo in training. The latter were dressed in their traditional long white tunics worn over loose-fitting white trousers and wearing pointed white hats that represent the mountain peaks. "We're experts in colonization," one of the Mamos said in Spanish. Daniel translated as he continued, "We've been colonized many times. Long ago, the Spanish conquistadors invaded us. Our ancestors fought them, but bows and arrows were no match for their weapons. They ripped apart the earth looking for gold, and they tried to make us Catholics. We said 'goodbye' to our beautiful ancestral lands, along the Caribbean Sea, and climbed higher into the mountains.

"Years later, the coffee and marijuana farmers arrived. At first, we tried to live with them, but they cut the forests, planted their bushes, poisoned the land with chemicals, and demanded that we change our ways, work on their farms. So, we moved higher. Then the cocaine drug lords, the police, the military, the guerrillas, and the CIA came. There was constant shooting. We retreated all the way up to the land of the glaciers."

The Mamo paused and studied the surrounding boulders. Turning back to us, he explained that part of his shamanic training had been to spend his childhood, from ages four to thirteen, living in a cave, talking and listening to the earth. "We understood that we'd been driven high into the mountains to learn, to hear the sad song of the melting glaciers. It was an opportunity for us to develop an even deeper connection with the earth. Now that peace has returned to this region, we are reclaiming our ancestral lands and making ourselves available to teach people like you how to behave. We are the Elder Siblings—our culture is older and wiser than yours. Our job is to show you, the Younger Siblings, about taking care of our sacred mother, the earth." He glanced around at the faces in our group. "We resisted colonization, but the minds of the Younger Siblings have been invaded with the ideas of the colonizers. We are here to change that."

As I sat there among those boulders, I thought about the jaguars the Kogi had faced. Rather than giving up, disheartened by the necessity of moving higher and higher into the mountains, they had embraced the opportunity to learn from the glaciers and the earth. They had created a new reality for themselves, that of teachers to the world.

"You actually lived in a cave for nine years?" someone asked the Mamo.

"Yes," he replied. "We learn to listen to the earth. When we listen, she speaks. Then we act."

It seemed that he was addressing another aspect of the modern world: a perception that stops us from truly listening—with our senses and our hearts. Although we have come to accept that the glaciers are melting and one hundred–year events like hurricanes happen every year or so, we couch these in pedantic reports and scientific measurements and postpone taking any real actions. The Kogi do not need a scientific report to state the obvious before acting.

We spent four days with the Kogi, hearing their stories and doing ceremonies with them. The latter included making offerings of gratitude to the earth—in their words, "the Great Mother"—giving thanks for all she provides for us. Each person left that group, like those in the other groups Daniel and I bring each year, deeply impressed by the simple lives of the Kogi, by their constant awareness of and gratitude for all that life and the earth give them, and by their determination to facilitate global change.

31

GOOD NEWS

I RETURN EVERY YEAR to lecture for a week at Tilton School, the New Hampshire boarding school where my dad taught. My parents and I lived in a house on campus where I'd spent the first eighteen years of my life. An all boys' tie-and-coat, highly regimented "prep" school then, it is now less formal and is coeducational.

After returning from that trip to the Kogi, I wandered the corridors of Plimpton Hall and inhaled the smell that I described to my dad when I was five years old as "polished-preppy-wood." I kept thinking about two men at Tilton who were among the most inspirational teachers I ever experienced: my sophomore English teacher, Richard Davis, and my junior history teacher, Jack Woodbury. Each man taught that history is changed by the written word—perception—more than by the sword. They also encouraged us to look for stories behind the official stories. Mr. Woodbury emphasized that history books are written by the victors and that the standard US story omits the facts behind a colonizing empire.

Stopping to peer through the glass window in a classroom door at students who were listening intently to their teacher, unaware of my presence, I wondered whether these students knew about the colonial aspects of American history. The actions the United States had taken to colonize a great many places, including Guam, the Panama Canal Zone, the Philippines, Puerto Rico, Samoa, and large areas of Mexico, and our efforts to control governments and economies in countries in Africa, Asia, Latin America, the Middle East, and Oceana are not things a nation that bills itself as a defender of democracy wants to include in its textbooks. But they are stories that need to be told so that we can touch the collective jaguar that has promoted the Death Economy.

I turned from the door and headed down the corridor. I made a mental note to talk about the relationship between US colonization and the Death Economy in my next lecture. A bell rang. Students rushed past. Classes had finished for the day. I continued on, lost in memories.

I ended up at my dad's old classroom, the place where at various times he taught Latin, Spanish, and French. A photograph of him as a handsome young man in a herringbone suit hung outside the door to that room, along with an inscription honoring his four decades at Tilton. I felt a deep sense of sadness, a longing to see him in person again, to hear his voice.

The room was empty. I entered and sat down in the chair behind the teacher's desk. I ran my hands along the dark wood, quite certain that it had been his desk. I sat quietly for a moment, feeling his presence. I recalled his telling me that the gladiator events I'd seen in a movie about ancient Rome were the sign of a decadent society, an empire in decline. I closed my eyes and was transported to the night I'd spent after taking ayahuasca at Taish's home.

A montage flashed before me of men brutalizing other men, women, and children—soldiers wielding swords and soldiers piloting drones that fired missiles that often killed civilians, heavy machinery ravaging the earth and belching poison into the air, homeless people wrapped in filthy blankets beneath elevated city highways, and opulent mansions high on terraced hills.

Then I saw the woman who had appeared at the end of that shamanic journey and again heard her voice: "The rich always want to get richer, consolidate their power. . . . Faithless dominators." And her final admonition: "You have work to do."

I opened my eyes and stared down at the top of my dad's desk. I knew as I sat there that the challenge for me was to once again touch my jaguar, to move past my own discouraging thoughts and fears of failure. I needed to accept the energy and the wisdom the jaguar offered. I needed to help others see how to change our narrative and ways of thinking, valuing, and acting.

I stood up and looked at a poster on the classroom wall. Versailles. We enjoy museums like Versailles today and marvel at the greed of kings who banqueted there while their subjects starved in the ghettoes outside. We ask ourselves how those kings could have justified such opulence in the midst of so much misery. And yet, all we need do is drive past the grandiose mansions, mega-yachts, and luxury jets of the current billionaires to ask ourselves similar questions.

I walked to the window. The sun was shining on the trees outside and, down the hill, on the New Hampshire town I used to know so well. How it had changed! Gone were the two grocery stores. The pharmacy. The magazine shop with the popular ice-cream-and-soda bar. The local bank. The two medical doctors' offices. The train station. Gone. All of them. There were a beauty salon and a few other small businesses, but Main Street now seemed like a ghost town to me.

From where I stood, I couldn't see the shopping malls that hadn't been there in my day, but I could visualize them over near the interstate that hadn't been there either. The town had lost its main businesses. But Tilton, the area, now offered shoppers from all over the state Walmart, Ralph Lauren, Banana Republic, Gap, Brooks Brothers, J. Crew, Coach, Nike . . .

I turned from that view back to the room. The current students at this school would witness changes that happen so rapidly and are so different from any humans have ever before experienced—or even imagined. I felt for the phone in my pocket. If any student in my day had suggested that we could read most of the information ever printed, hear music, watch movies and TV shows, do our shopping and banking, and enjoy instant communications with people all over our planet on such a tiny device, we would have laughed him out of the room.

As my fingers played with that phone, some good news occurred to me. Despite all the problems we confront today, we also now have access to information that can shake us awake and motivate us to change. The long march of hierarchical, colonial history has led us to this moment of awareness. We are learning that the melting glaciers, species extinctions, political turmoil, and other heart-wrenching events are symptoms of a global social-governmental-economic system that is consuming itself into extinction. A dying economy, a Death Economy, it is based on an assumption that success is defined by the maximization of short-term profits for corporations and short-term accumulation of material things for individuals, regardless of the environmental and social costs.

I looked again at the poster of Versailles, a symbol of the determination of the rich to maintain their power throughout the ages. I'd spent a large share of my life as part of that legacy, a modern-day soldier-colonist who used a combination of fear and debt to spread a system that I'd thought was capitalism, only to finally discover that it is an aberrant, predatory, monopolistic form that mocks capitalism.* I and my cohorts stifled competition, overthrew democratic governments, and promoted xenophobic nationalism whenever those things served the purpose of Big Business. Now, standing in that classroom, I knew that things would change. One way or another.

When enough of us confront the jaguar that is our fear of change, this Death Economy will be transformed into one that cleans up pollution, regenerates destroyed environments, and creates technologies that do not ravage the environment, a living economy, a Life Economy. Otherwise, we will meet with ever increasing catastrophes. We will either change our ideas, values, and actions and accept new ways of relating to other people, resources, countries, governments, and cultures, or we will propel ourselves into extinction—or something unimaginably close to extinction.

I pushed myself up from Dad's chair and walked out of his room to the familiar smell of polished-preppy-wood. Slowly, I moved along the corridor, down the stairs, and outside. Across the campus was the small white-washed house where I'd lived with my parents. Although it was now the home of another teacher, it looked the same. I imagined Mom standing on the steps, waving at me.

I thought of the times she'd experienced: the Great Depression, Hitler, Pearl Harbor, and World War II. But times got better. The Depression ended. The Germans and Japanese surrendered. Our former enemies became our friends.

An image came to mind of my nine-year-old grandson, Grant, the great-grandson Mom and Dad never lived to meet. He was an inspiration

---

* For details on predatory capitalism and the Death and Life Economies, see the Resources section.

to me, a very immediate motivation for doing the work I knew I had to do. My grandparents and parents had brought us through terrible crises. It was our job to help prepare the generations represented by the students at this school and Grant to face the challenges yet to come.

I glanced around at the dormitories, the sidewalks, and the tree-lined lawns. I thought about how much I'd learned during my life. I thought about the various venues in the different countries where I give talks, from a business school in China to a music festival in the Czech Republic, from an international economic summit in Russia to meetings of conscious capitalists in the US, from a yoga retreat center in the Bahamas to a conference of corporate CEOs in Turkey, and so many others. I recalled discussions I've had with CEOs who've told me they want their companies to be much more socially and environmentally responsible. However, they fear that if they lose market share or their stock price falls, they will be fired and replaced by someone who cares only about market share or stock prices. Several of these CEOs have urged me to ask audiences to start social networking campaigns that flood them with messages such as "We love your product but we won't buy it anymore until you pay your overseas workers a living wage (use only recycled materials, and so on)." They can then take these messages to their boards of directors and fight for the changes they themselves want to see. One CEO told me, "Even sociopathic executives will join the green movement if that, instead of short-term profits, becomes the measure of success."

I thought about the incredible progress that the Pachamama Alliance has made since those days back in 1995 when that small group met with the Achuar people, and I thought about all the places I go where there are Pachamama Alliance people organizing and working to shift the destructive patterns of modern civilizations. It has become apparent that around the planet, more and more people understand the need for change. They are confused as to what to do. Some embrace right-wing governments. Others turn to the left. But people from very diverse political and cultural leanings are realizing that the current systems aren't serving us anymore. That realization is the first step toward change.

I flashed back to the newspaper photo of that shrunken head I'd seen on my first flight to Ecuador. And the terrifying moment when my plane was attacked by Achuar warriors. I thought about the Amazonian nations, people who had killed each other for centuries and then had come together to take unified actions to protect their territories. They had confronted that which they most feared, us in the modern world.

That day at Tilton School had a lasting impact on me. It helped me understand that we know we must address the problems of climate change, war, world hunger, deforestation, and so much more, but we ignore the fact that all of these are symptoms, that the Death Economy is the disease. The jaguar seems to block us from overcoming our belief that we can't change anything that big. Instead of acting, we tell ourselves that we're too weak, too inadequate, too insignificant, or too comfortable.

Then I realized that the jaguar that seems to block us actually wants us to touch it so it can give us the power to turn things around. If such monumental changes as the uniting of former enemies in the Amazon and after World War II can happen, then people today are certainly capable of coming together to solve some of the gravest problems humans have ever faced, those that confront us right now. Whether we live in Korea, Afghanistan, Yemen, Russia, China, America, or some other country, we are, first and foremost, citizens of the world. We are smart enough to stop the shortsighted divisiveness and instead unite to protect our common territory, our Living Earth, the only home we have.

There is one very important objective reality: the world is blessed with abundant human and natural resources. A Perception Bridge determines the way we relate to that reality. When we buy into the perception that we must use those resources to maximize short-term materialistic gains, regardless of the environmental and social costs, we cross to a Death Economy. But if we open ourselves to the perception that we can utilize those same resources to create systems that are sustainable, renewable, and regenerative, we cross to a Life Economy. A jaguar stands on that bridge. It is time to end our fear of change and instead embrace the powers for change the jaguar offers, break through the mind-sets that have burdened us with failing systems, and apply the human and natural resources to create systems that will be successful for generations to come.

Conclusion

THE JAGUAR'S MESSAGE

In these tracks, feel the jaguar that blocks your people. And feel the jaguar that is your ally for change.

FIVE DECADES AFTER I FIRST entered the Amazon rain forest, I was back there on another Pachamama Alliance trip. I was paddling a two-person kayak up the Capahuari River near the Kapawi Lodge with a woman who went simply by the name "Z."

She broke the silence. "There's something swimming in the river."

"Probably that tapir one of the Achuar saw near here yesterday."

Z turned to me. "No," she whispered. "It's a jaguar!"

I froze, my paddle suspended above the kayak. My heart raced. Slowly, cautiously, I lowered the paddle to rest on the kayak and leaned forward to peer around her.

A band of white water cut across the river, the wake of something swimming. I raised a hand to shade my eyes and followed the white water. Then I saw it: the black-spotted tawny-colored head and shoulders of a full-grown jaguar, just yards ahead of us, swimming to the river bank. Our momentum was taking us rapidly toward it. I grabbed the paddle and stopped the canoe's forward motion.

Speechless, we sat there, still, quiet, watching.

Without breaking its rhythm, the jaguar turned and looked at us; then it continued to the shore, climbed out of the water, shook itself, gave us another glance, bounded up the embankment, and disappeared into the tangle of foliage.

A flock of terrified turkey-sized *hoatzin* birds flew out of the trees and over the river, desperate to escape.

Later that day, a group of Achuar men took me in their dugout canoe to show them the place where the jaguar had left the river. Sitting behind me was one of the men who years before had attacked our plane and tried to kill Yahanua because she was Shuar. He now had a Shuar wife. Symbolic of the changing times, intermarriage between these two cultures, fierce enemies for hundreds of years, had now become common. They had truly touched their jaguars.

The canoe arrived at the muddy bank of the river. One by one, the Achuar stepped out and placed their hands on the jaguar's claw marks.

"We're touching the jaguar," one of them, the youngest, said, laughing. He helped me from the canoe and encouraged me to lay my hands on the prints. "In these tracks, feel the jaguar that blocks your people," he advised. "And feel the jaguar that is your ally for change."

After we returned to the canoe, I asked what he meant by that.

"A jaguar appears to block your people from changing, from stopping actions that are destroying these forests—and the world. However, that jaguar also offers to give you the power to change."

Those words were so familiar and yet at that moment they seemed more significant than ever before. Perhaps it was the fact that I had just come very close to a real jaguar and had touched its tracks that impacted me, or perhaps it was the voice of the young Achuar man. Whatever it was, it reminded me of the descriptions I'd read of ancient cultures that honored the jaguar for its valor, physical strength, and mental awareness. I thought of the Achuar who today see the jaguar as a symbol that encourages us to face our fears, break through barriers, and determine our paths to the future. I thought about the Eagle and the Condor Prophecy, the Mayan Prophecy of 2012, and the Shuar Legend of Etsaa and the Evias. And about the recent unification of Amazonian peoples. Every one of these stories and events emphasizes the power we humans have to alter reality by changing perceptions and taking new actions.

Sitting in that Achuar canoe, I understood that these stories had come to the modern industrialized world at a time when confronting our fears and turning them into actions that create personal and global change is essential to our survival.

As our canoe continued down the river toward the lodge, I turned once again to glance at the Achuar men seated behind me. Then I looked at the magnificent forests around us. A seed had been planted here by these people in this forest just a little more than two decades earlier. It was a seed of hope, one that carries a message about the power we have when we come together to protect our homeland, our Living Earth. That seed has taken root and the roots are spreading across the planet.

RESOURCES

WHAT YOU CAN DO

NEVER BEFORE HAS IT BEEN MORE IMPORTANT to alter the course of history. Never has there been a time when global communications could offer such great opportunities for change. Events like the creation of the internet and mobile phones have enabled us to expand our knowledge about our planet and ourselves and to participate in movements that change our policies and actions. Social networks empower us to join together to let corporations know that if they want us to work for, buy from, and invest in them, they will have to commit to a Life Economy.

There are many indicators that we have the ability to change powerful institutions. Political initiatives such as the Green New Deal; movements like conscious capitalism; innovative approaches to business that include B Corporations, benefit corporations,* cooperatives, and local banks; alternative energy technologies and approaches to organic farming; programs like Drawdown; and the creation of the Long-Term Stock Exchange are just a few examples. The August 2019 Business Roundtable meeting was a highly significant signal of impending change; CEOs from 192 of some of the world's largest corporations promised to "abandon the idea that companies must maximize profits for shareholders above all else" and instead

---

* The publisher of this book is both a B Corporation (a certification that it meets rigorous standards of social and environmental responsibility, accountability, and transparency) and a benefit corporation (a legal status obligating it to be operated for the benefit of all of its stakeholders, not just its shareholders).

"commit to balancing the need of shareholders with customers, employees, suppliers and local communities.'" Although this promise, like the other indicators, was a confirmation that concepts in business are changing, it is up to each of us to use social media and whatever other means are available to us to demand that these corporations, as well as the governments that support them, take actions to honor their commitments.

At this critical moment in human evolution, we are challenged to manifest the Mayan Prophecy, the Eagle and the Condor Prophecy, and many other stories that encourage us to rise to a new level of consciousness. We are challenged to confront the Evias that are cannibalizing our environment, resources, and minds; to take actions that reverse long-standing destructive social, political, environmental, and economic patterns; and to learn from Indigenous peoples the importance of abandoning colonizing attitudes that create destructive realities. We are challenged to unite cultures and countries in a common cause to make our homeland, the earth, a place that remains habitable.

You arrived at this critical moment to help meet these challenges. The fact that you've read this far indicates that you are ready to do your part. When you ask, "What can I do?" you invite yourself to touch your jaguar and gather the courage, creativity, and wisdom needed to take actions that will alter reality for yourself and the planet.

The answer to "What can I do?" is you can change yourself and the world. A good place to start is to ask yourself a few more questions:

1. **Who and what am I?**

   - Why was I born at this critical time in history into the situation and society that raised me?

   - What is my mission in life, my highest purpose, that which will bring me joy and make me feel good about myself?

   - Who or what has been colonized in me?

2. **What are my jaguars, my fears?**

   - What stands in the way of my mission in life, my highest purpose, my greatest joy?

- What barriers does the fact that I am (name your race, your background, your prejudices, and other things you know about yourself) create for me?

- What thoughts, prejudices, biases, and traits are holding me back from making the changes I want to make—in me, my family, my community, my nation, the world?

- What perceived weaknesses do I need to overcome?

3. How do I confront my jaguars and alter my perceptions?

- What are the first steps I need to take to manifest my mission, my higher purpose?

- What specifically do I need to do to break through the barriers that have held me back?

- How do I alter perceptions about the traits that in the past I've seen as negative or as weaknesses and allow them to help me move forward?

- What new perceptions about me and my life do I need to embrace?

4. What actions do I take for me personally?

- What are my passions and skills? How can I use them to take actions that will bring me joy and propel me to my mission?

- What gifts can the jaguar give me so that I can use my passions and skills to create the me I most respect and want to be?

- What do I know about Indigenous people and their cultures that can help me better understand the actions necessary to unite my family, my community, my nation, the world?

5. How do *I* change the world?

- How can I learn to look at the world through Indigenous eyes, understanding that the smallest insect and the largest tree are as necessary to the earth's survival as the tiniest cell and largest organ in my body are to my survival?

- How can I help businesses commit to a Life Economy, especially those where my friends and I shop, work, learn the news, and invest our money?

- What types of wisdom, strength, and motivation can the jaguar give me that will empower me to do that?

- What will it take for me to cross the Perception Bridge from supporting a Death Economy to playing my part in facilitating a Life Economy?

- What can I do to decolonize the world?

To integrate these questions into your daily life and map out actions to take, you can do the following:

1. Offer yourself a practice that is relaxing, inspiring, empowering, and fun. This might be meditation, yoga, shamanic journeying, walking in the woods, or any number of activities. (An example of a daily practice follows.) The key is to use this practice to inspire yourself to ask questions like the ones we just covered, embrace the answers with your heart and mind, and act accordingly.

2. Tell the new story, the powerful story about the need to accept new values and create a Life Economy. When someone around you complains about how bad things are—or when you yourself are tempted to complain—turn that around, find a positive story. Stories speak louder than facts alone and are heard without the resistance that often accompanies attempts to argue people into agreement. Keep an eye out for the good news that is happening (solar and wind energy, technologies that collect plastics in the oceans and recycle them, supermarkets that sell organic and locally grown produce, CEOs whose actions support the Business Roundtable's commitment, etc.). Even if at first you're tempted to brush some stories off as "just marketing propaganda," know that telling such stories changes perceptions (e.g., the slave-owning Thomas Jefferson, whose words in the Declaration of Independence changed perceptions about slavery; a woman who confessed that she started hanging her clothes to dry on an outdoor line to

impress her neighbors and has since realized that it was the first step to becoming a leader in energy-conservation movements). Spread the good news to all your friends and networks. Encourage those who take a first step—regardless of their motives—to take a second step, and then a third . . .

3. Recognize that being truly you and participating in creating a Life Economy is the most rewarding and joy-filled thing you will ever do!

The following is one example of a practice that can help you accomplish these suggestions.

EXAMPLE OF A DAILY PRACTICE

Five steps to a happier life and better world

1. Define your dream, your greatest desire, a life that will bring you the most happiness (e.g., "I want to write books," "I want to make a living as a yoga teacher," "I want to work with my hands and wood as a carpenter").

2. In one sentence, describe how your dream can support a Life Economy ("I will write Life Economy–supporting stories," "I will use yoga to inspire my clients to dare to change themselves and the world," "I will employ sustainable materials and let my clients know that they're investing in the future").

3. In one sentence, identify a jaguar that blocks you from realizing your dream ("I don't have time to write," "People don't go to yoga to change the world," "It's not appropriate for me, a carpenter, to talk to my clients about the future").

4. In one sentence, commit to touching that jaguar ("I will get up a little earlier every morning and write for half an hour," "I can help yoga practitioners understand that change is essential," "Carpentry is all about building for the future").

5. Read all four of the previous steps to yourself every morning and take daily actions to make them happen (write for half an hour, start talking to your yoga students or carpentry clients about change and the future). Expand upon these as needed. The important thing: do

something every single day that advances your dream for a happier life for you and a better world for all.

HINT: Daily actions can take many forms, ranging from the simple (tweeting) to the complex (running for public office) and just about everything in between. An example of something simple that requires very little time and effort: You can identify a company that you feel should become more socially or environmentally responsible and start (or join) a social networking campaign. Urge all your social network circles to send that company a message such as "We love your product but we won't buy it anymore until you _____ (fill in the blank with whatever it is you want the company to do)." Ask everyone in your circles to send that message to their circles. Know that you are supporting those people in the company who want change (there are lots in every company); they can use these messages to convince their bosses and boards of directors that they must change if they want to keep their customers.

Now you are ready to touch the jaguar and transform your fears into actions to change the world.

DEATH VERSUS LIFE ECONOMIES

There is a major difference between capitalism and what many economists refer to as "predatory capitalism," a deviant that has little in common with the original. According to *Merriam-Webster*, capitalism is

> *An economic system characterized by private or corporate ownership of capital goods, by investments that are determined by private decision, and by prices, production, and the distribution of goods that are determined mainly by competition in a free market.*[2]

The *Oxford Dictionary* defines it as

> *An economic and political system in which a country's trade and industry are controlled by private owners for profit, rather than by the state.*[3]

Today's Death Economy is a far cry from either of these definitions. It is characterized by businesses that destroy or absorb their competition and oppose free market policies. Not only does the state not own businesses; businesses and their billionaire shareholders control the state. It is a predatory aberrant—that actually should not be considered capitalism.

The Death Economy is driven by the goal that was promoted by a group of economists in the 1970s and 1980s, including Nobel Prize winners Friedrich von Hayek (1974) and Milton Friedman (1976), and can be summarized as "the only responsibility of business is to maximize short-term owner profits, regardless of the social and environmental costs."

The stories that accompany this perception give corporate executives the right—even the mandate—to do whatever they think it will take to maximize profits, including buying public officials through campaign financing and promises of lucrative post-government consulting or lobbying jobs; exploiting workers; annihilating or buying out their competitors; destroying environments; reducing taxes and wages; lobbying against pro-worker, pro-consumer, and pro-ecology regulations; promising (as well as threatening) to impact economies by locating their facilities in (or removing them from) cities and countries; and depleting the very resources upon which the long-term survival of their businesses depends. These stories promote top-down, authoritarian chains of command and autocratic management styles—in government as well as business.

KEY CHARACTERISTICS OF THE DEATH ECONOMY

- Its goal is to maximize short-term profits for a relative few.
- It uses fear and debt to gain market share and political control.
- It promotes the idea that for someone to win, another must lose.
- It is predatory, encouraging businesses to prey on each other, people, and the environment.
- It destroys resources needed for its own long-term survival.
- It values goods and services that are "extractive" and materialistic above those that enhance quality of life (e.g., child-rearing, the arts).

- It is heavily influenced by nonproductive financial deals (stock manipulation, financialization, "gambling").

- It ignores externalities, such as environmental destruction and exploitation of workers, when measuring profits, GDP, and other metrics.

- It invests heavily in militarization—in killing, or threatening to kill, people and other life-forms and destroying infrastructure.

- It causes pollution, environmental collapse, and drastic income and social inequality and may lead to political instability.

- It vilifies taxes, rather than defining them as investments (in social services, infrastructure, the military, etc.).

- It is undemocratic, encouraging the growth of large corporations controlled by a few individuals whose money has a strong influence on politics (monopolies that lead to oligarchies).

- It is based on top-down, authoritarian chains of command that support autocratic management styles—in business and government.

- It places higher values on nonproductive jobs (venture capitalists, investment bankers) than productive ones (laborers, factory workers) and those that enrich life (teachers, musicians, artists).

- It keeps billions of people in poverty.

- It classifies plants, animals, and the entire natural world as depletable resources; fails to respect and protect nature; and causes massive extinctions and other irreversible problems.

- It has become the predominant advocate of what it calls "capitalism" around the world.

The future lies in transforming the Death Economy into a Life Economy that cleans up pollution, regenerates devastated ecosystems, recycles, and develops technologies that restore resources and that benefit, rather than ravage, the environment. Businesses that pay returns to investors who invest in an economy that is itself a renewable resource become the success stories.

The Life Economy is driven by the goal of maximizing long-term benefits for all life and the environment.

KEY CHARACTERISTICS OF THE LIFE ECONOMY

- Its goal is to serve a public interest (maximize long-term benefits for people and nature).

- Its laws support level playing fields that encourage healthy non-monopolistic competition, innovative ideas, and sustainable products.

- It embraces a sense of cooperation, the idea that we all can win when we set our goals for long-term benefits for all.

- It values quality of life and spiritually enhancing activities above those based solely on materialism and extraction.

- It is based on beneficially productive activities, such as recycling, education, health care, and the arts, rather than the nonproductive, such as stock manipulation, financialization, and "gambling."

- It cleans up pollution.

- It regenerates devastated environments.

- It is driven by compassion and debt avoidance.

- It helps hungry people feed themselves.

- It includes externalities in its financial and economic measurements.

- It innovates—develops and embraces new, regenerative, sustainable technologies.

- It recycles.

- It defines taxes as investments (should your tax monies be invested in health care or militarization?).

- It is democratic, encouraging locally based commerce and employee- or community-owned businesses that benefit many (e.g., cooperatives, B Corporations, etc.).

- It reinforces democratic decision-making processes and management styles—in business and government.

- It places a high value on jobs that enrich life (musicians, social and medical workers, parents).

- It is based on a foundational knowledge that humans are in a symbiotic relationship with our planet, that we must respect, honor, and protect the natural world.

- It rewards investors who support all the previous characteristics.

- It was the predominant form of economic evolution for much of the two hundred thousand years of human history.

The transition happens through changes in the perceptions that drive values and actions and the stories we tell around them. "Maximize short-term profits for a few, regardless of the social and environmental costs" becomes "maximize long-term benefits for all people and nature." When groups of consumers, workers, and investors accept these values and take actions to support businesses that promote them and pressure governments to codify them into laws, the change we want and need happens.

It is happening. We all need to encourage it to happen faster.

NOTES

PROLOGUE

1   John Perkins, *Confessions of an Economic Hit Man* (San Francisco: Berrett-Koehler, 2004), ix.

2   (a) Kate Doyle and Carlos Osorio, "U.S. Policy in Guatemala, 1966–1996," National Security Archive Electronic Briefing Book No. 11, The National Security Archive, The George Washington University, 2013, accessed November 23, 2019, https://nsarchive2 .gwu.edu/NSAEBB/NSAEBB11/docs/.

(b) "Guatemalan Civil War," Wikipedia, accessed November 23, 2019, https://en .wikipedia.org/wiki/Guatemalan_Civil_War.

3   (a) "Peeling Back the Truth on Guatemalan Bananas," Council on Hemispheric Affairs, July 28, 2010, accessed November 23, 2019, http://www.coha.org/peeling-back-the -truth-on-the-guatemalan-banana-industry/.

(b) Rachel Nolan, "A Translation Crisis at the Border," *New Yorker*, January 6, 2020, Annals of Immigration, https://www.newyorker.com/magazine/2020/01/06/a -translation-crisis-at-the-border.

CHAPTER 1

1   Bob Orkland, "I Ain't Got No Quarrel with Them Vietcong," opinion, *New York Times*, June 27, 2017, accessed November 23, 2019, https://www.nytimes.com/2017/06/27 /opinion/muhammad-ali-vietnam-war.html.

CHAPTER 2

1   "Ayahuasca Shows Promise in Treating Addiction and PTSD," *Psychedelic Times*, accessed October 23, 2019, https://psychedelictimes.com/learn-more-ayahuasca/.

CHAPTER 10

1   For details, see John Perkins, *The Secret History of the American Empire* (New York: Plume, 2017), 85–93.

CHAPTER 13

1   Lynne Twist, *The Soul of Money* (New York: W.W. Norton, 2003), 174–175.

CHAPTER 18

1   Lynne Twist, *The Soul of Money* (New York: W.W. Norton, 2003), 177.

CHAPTER 24

1   Lynne Twist, *The Soul of Money* (New York: W.W. Norton, 2003), 178.

CHAPTER 29

1   "Early Success with Our Indigenous Partners" and "Educating, Inspiring, and Guiding People Into Action," Origin Story, Pachamama Alliance, accessed November 24, 2019, https://www.pachamama.org/about/origin.

RESOURCES

1   Jenna McGregor, "Group of Top CEOs Says Maximizing Shareholder Profits No Longer Can Be the Primary Goal of Corporations," *Washington Post*, August 19, 2019, accessed November 23, 2019, https://www.washingtonpost.com/business/2019 /08/19/lobbying-group-powerful-ceos-is-rethinking-how-it-defines-corporations -purpose/?noredirect=on.

2   *Merriam-Webster*, s.v. "capitalism," accessed November 23, 2019, https://www.merriam -webster.com/dictionary/capitalism.

3   Lexico, s.v. "capitalism," accessed November 23, 2019, https://www.lexico.com/en /definition/capitalism.

AUTHOR'S COMMENT AND ACKNOWLEDGMENTS

THIS BOOK IS NONFICTION. All the events described in these pages actually happened. I wanted to capture the feelings around the situations described, to make the book an exciting read as well as a source of information and inspiration. Therefore, I chose a literary form known as narrative nonfiction—as I had in my earlier books.

One of the challenges of narrative nonfiction is the protection of people who might feel threatened by the exposure of their identities. Readers of my previous books on Indigenous cultures—those written in the 1980s and 1990s—may note that I have sometimes used names and described the details of situations slightly differently in this one. I felt compelled in former times to mask the identities of some individuals and to modify details around incidents concerning shamans and Indigenous traditions. Times and attitudes have changed a great deal during the past decades. Shamanic practices are widely accepted. I do not feel the same need to disguise identities or traditions now as I did in the past. Therefore, with a few exceptions, the names of people and places in this book are the actual ones. One exception is that I sometimes use pronouns ("he" and "she") instead of names for trip participants.

Whenever I re-create events or conversations, I rely on personal records, notes, and recollections. In quoting people, I make every attempt to reflect the meaning of what they said and their feelings, rather than trying to repeat the exact words. In some cases, I combine several incidents or dialogues into one to facilitate the flow of the narrative. It is always interesting to listen to recordings of conversations and to note the many times we repeat ourselves, stumble over words, and insert sounds like "hmmm" and "ah" and phrases like "I mean." That is the way we talk, but it makes for boring reading!

I am so very grateful to the many people whose lives I've shared and who are identified by name in these pages. This book would not have been written without them. Since their names and their contribution to this narrative have already been described, I'll not mention them here.

My deepest thanks go to the Maya, Shuar, Achuar, Sapara, Kichwa, and Kogi people, who have been my teachers and my inspiration. Among the individuals whose names are not mentioned, I am especially grateful to shamans like Manari Ushigua, Tata Julio Tot, Tata Domingo Bolom Xi, Nana Ernestina Reyes, Tata Marco Antonio Ramos, Mamo Alejandro Nieves, Mamo Lorenzo Pinto, Mamo Vicente, Mamo Marco, Juan Nieves, Manuel Dingula, Jaruen Rodriguez, Lucy Perez, Seinake Rodriguez, Sumpa, Tunduama, Chumpi, and Daniel Wachapa and to community leaders like Luis Vargas, Domingo Peas, Santiago Kawarim, Luis Kawarim, TIo Walter, and Ramiro Vargas, who played important roles in forging the partnership that is the Pachamama Alliance, as well as to the many men and women who continue to support that partnership.

Since the beginning, the Pachamama Alliance has been empowered by early board members, Tracy Apple, Neal Rogan, Gordon Starr, and Bob Curtis; the many other remarkable board members who joined us later; an absolutely incredible Pachamama Alliance staff (who prefer to be called "the team"); and all the thousands of people across the globe who have helped us in so many ways. They are changing the dream of the modern world and preserving the rain forest that is vital to life as we know it. My deepest gratitude goes out to all of them.

Berrett-Koehler founder and brilliant editor, Steve Piersanti, encouraged and coached me through the writing and publishing process. I can't begin to express the profound appreciation I feel for him and for all the BK staff, especially the Editorial, Design and Production, Sales and Marketing, and International Sales and Subsidiary Rights departments. I love working with BK and am deeply inspired by so many dedicated and highly talented individuals there. I love the fact that BK is a B Corporation and a benefit corporation that walks its talk.

AUTHOR'S COMMENT AND ACKNOWLEDGMENTS

I am forever grateful to Robert Rosenthal, an award-winning journalist whose illustrious career includes being on *The New York Times* team that produced the Pentagon Papers, Editor of *The Philadelphia Inquirer*, Managing Editor of *The San Francisco Chronicle*, and Executive Director of The Center for Investigative Reporting. Like the thorough reporter he is, Robert read my previous books and encouraged me to expand on details about many of my experiences, especially those in the Amazon. His brilliance and talents helped me develop and wordsmith many of the ideas expressed in this book.

A special thanks to the people who read and critiqued draft versions of *Touching the Jaguar*: Stephan Rechtschaffen, Kiman Lucas, Sheila Mitchel, David Korten, Rachel Henry, and Rachel Neumann. Their insights and recommendations inspired me to take the book to new levels. I am especially grateful to BK's Jeevan Sivasubramaniam for organizing some of these readers; to Danielle Scott Goodman for going beyond her job as a reader and offering extremely valuable advice around socially and culturally sensitive issues; to Susan Berge who took on the tough job of making final edits, was courageous enough to support my desire to sometimes side-step stylistic "requirements" in the name of making the text more exciting, and who worked with me as a team member to complete everything on time; to Maureen Forys, designer and compositor extraordinaire; and to Killian Lucas and Jessica Scheer who round out the team with their brilliance and technical skills for developing websites and communicating ideas expressed in the book through social networking channels. The comments and suggestions from this group of very talented people helped me mold this book into one that I believe and hope is a fun read, as well as an inspiration for you, the reader, to touch your jaguars and change your life and the world.

INDEX

ABOUT THE AUTHOR

JOHN PERKINS has lived four lives: (1) as an economic hit man (EHM); (2) as the CEO of a successful alternative energy company, where he was rewarded for not disclosing his EHM past; (3) as an expert on Indigenous cultures and shamanism, who applied this expertise to promoting good stewardship of the planet; and (4) as a writer and an activist who told the real-life story about his extraordinary dealings as an EHM and exposed the international intrigue and corruption that turned the US into a global empire.

Now John writes about how these four lives are linked. *Touching the Jaguar* is a bridge connecting the world of the EHM and the corporate executive to the world of the shaman and the activist. It delves into the problems that current greed and short-term perspectives are causing and offers ways to solve them. It presents actions that readers can take to change their lives, convert a "Death Economy" into a "Life Economy," and help make the world a place future generations will want to inherit.

HISTORY

As an EHM, John's job was to persuade economically developing countries to accept enormous loans for infrastructure development and to guarantee that the development projects would be contracted to US corporations. Once these countries were saddled with debts, the US government and the international aid agencies allied with it were able to control the countries' economies and to ensure that oil and other resources were channeled to serve the interests of building a global empire.

John traveled all over the world and was a participant in some of the most dramatic events in modern history, including the Saudi Arabian money-laundering affair, the rise and fall of the shah of Iran, the deaths of Ecuador's and Panama's heads of state, the subsequent invasion of Panama, the inception of terrorist groups in Colombia, and events leading up to the current turmoil in the Middle East.

In 1980, John founded Independent Power Systems Inc. (IPS), a company dedicated to developing environmentally beneficial energy projects. Under his leadership as CEO, IPS became an extremely successful firm in a high-risk business where most of its competitors failed. Many "coincidences" and favors from people in powerful positions helped make IPS an industry leader. John also served as a highly paid consultant to some of the corporations whose pockets he had previously helped line. He took on this role in response to threats on his life and also lucrative payoffs—the same "carrot and stick" techniques he had used to convince country leaders to play the EHM game.

Although John had learned in business school that the EHM model was the best model for economic development, he came to understand that it was a new form of colonialism. Returning to the Amazon, he saw the destructive impact of his work, and he was struck by the example of a previously uncontacted Amazonian tribe that touched its jaguar by uniting with age-old enemies to defend its territory against invading oil and mining companies.

John sold IPS in 1990 and became a champion for Indigenous rights and environmental movements. He worked closely with Amazonian nations to help them preserve their rain forests. He wrote five books, published in many languages, about Indigenous cultures, shamanism, ecology, and sustainability; taught at universities and learning centers on four continents; and founded and served on the board of directors of several leading nonprofit organizations.

Then came September 11, 2001. The terrible events of that day led John to drop the veil of secrecy around his life as an EHM. He ignored the threats and bribes and wrote *Confessions of an Economic Hit Man*. In doing so, he shared his insider knowledge about the role that the US government, multinational "aid" organizations, and corporations have played in bringing the world to a place where such an event could occur. He felt that he owed this to his country, to his daughter, to all the people around the world who suffer because of the work he and his peers have done, and to himself. In this book, he outlined the dangerous path his country is taking as it moves away from the original ideals of the American republic and toward global empire.

THE MESSAGE

Two of the nonprofit organizations John founded or cofounded, the Pachamama Alliance and Dream Change, have become models for inspiring people to make a better world, empowering individuals to create more environmentally sustainable, socially just, and balanced communities. These organizations also have played major roles in helping Amazonian people protect their lands and cultures against the devastation caused by oil, mining, and other "development" projects. John assuaged some of the guilt he felt over his EHM work by applying to his nonprofit work and writing profession much of the money he earned as a consultant and author.

Confessions of an Economic Hit Man became an international bestseller. It spent more than seventy weeks on the *New York Times* bestseller list and launched John on a global speaking tour that has continued ever since.

In *The New Confessions of an Economic Hit Man*, John exposed the fact that EHMs had become more ubiquitous and dangerous in the twelve years since the publication of the original book. He explained that the modern form of capitalism, known as predatory capitalism, has created a system that is consuming itself into self-destruction, a "Death Economy."

John's books have sold more than two million copies and been published in more than thirty-five languages. He has taken worldwide his message of the need to replace the Death Economy with a Life Economy that is itself a renewable resource and that cleans up pollution, regenerates devastated environments, and develops resource-protective technologies.

He speaks in countries around the world at many different venues and to a variety of audiences, including at corporate summits, to large groups of CEOs and other business leaders, and at shamanic gatherings, consumer conferences, and music festivals.

John has taught or lectured at Harvard, Oxford, and more than fifty other universities; been featured on ABC, NBC, CNN, CNBC, NPR, A&E, and the History Channel; been written up in *Time*, the *New York Times*, the *Washington Post*, *Cosmopolitan*, *Elle*, *Der Spiegel*, and many other publications; and appeared in numerous documentaries, including *The End of Poverty?*, *Zeitgeist Addendum*, and *Apology of an Economic Hit Man*. A&E featured him in a special titled "Headhunters of the Amazon," narrated by Leonard Nimoy. *Time* magazine selected Dream Change as one of the thirteen organizations in the world whose websites best reflect the ideals and goals of Earth Day. He was awarded the Lennon Ono Grant for Peace and the Rainforest Action Network Challenging Business As Usual Award.

John's books on global economics and intrigue, in addition to the two *Confessions* books, include *The Secret History of the American Empire* (Penguin) and *Hoodwinked* (Random House). His books on Indigenous cultures and transformation include *Shapeshifting*, *The World Is As You Dream It*, *Psychonavigation*, *Spirit of the Shuar*, and *The Stress-Free Habit* (all from Inner Traditions International—Bear & Company).

CONTACTING AND MEETING THE AUTHOR

To join John on trips to the Indigenous people described in this book, subscribe to his newsletter, and meet him at various venues where he speaks and gives workshops, please visit www.johnperkins.org. Connect with John on Facebook at facebook.com/johnperkinsauthor, on Instagram at @johnperkinsauthor, and on Twitter at @economic_hitman.

To discover more about the work of the Pachamama Alliance and Dream Change, two of his nonprofit 501(c) organizations, please visit www.pachamama.org and www.dreamchange.org.

ABOUT THE PACHAMAMA ALLIANCE

WE ARE GRATEFUL to our cofounder, John Perkins, for sharing our remarkable story and for donating a portion of the revenues of this book to our organization.

The Pachamama Alliance is a global community of people dedicated to bringing about an environmentally sustainable, spiritually fulfilling, socially just human presence on this planet, and we invite you to join us.

We are a unique organization with a dual mission: to empower the Indigenous people of the Amazon rain forest to preserve their lands and cultures and, using insights gained from that relationship, to educate and inspire individuals everywhere to take action to bring forth a thriving, just, and sustainable future.

Our focus is on enabling individuals and communities to engage in meaningful, measurable action that **reverses global warming and restores** our planet's living systems.

Our **Sacred Headwaters Initiative** works with Indigenous nations in the rainforests of Ecuador and Peru to permanently protect nearly seventy million acres of the world's most biodiverse ecosystem from destructive extractive industries. This powerful initiative not only protects this vital ecosystem but also ensures sustainable, dignified livelihoods for its Indigenous people.

Our work throughout the rest of the world brings the Indigenous perspective to bear on our mounting global crises. Through our transformational educational programs, we seek to "change the dream of the modern world"—a dream rooted in consumerism and separation that is creating the Death Economy described in this book. Our educational programs are available online and in person in several languages and in more than

80 countries and facilitate the transformation of the Death Economy to a Life Economy.

We also offer other live and online programs:

Pachamama Journeys take you on extraordinary trips to visit the cultures and shamans introduced in this book. You're invited to go on a life-changing journey to the most biodiverse ecosystem in the world: the sacred headwaters of the Amazon.

Awakening the Dreamer is a multimedia workshop that dives into the causes of and solutions to our current environmental, social, and spiritual crises and shifts perceptions from apathy and resignation to possibility and engagement.

The Game Changer Intensive is an eight-week online course that will educate, inspire, and equip you to be a *pro*-activist leader—a game changer in your community.

Pachamama Alliance Communities are local groups of people committed to sharing our work in more than fifty locations in the US and in several other countries.

The Global Commons is our online community where you get news and information about our work and participate in lively conversations and webinars.

For more information about all of these opportunities, explore our website, Pachamama.org.

Also by John Perkins

The New Confessions of an Economic Hit Man

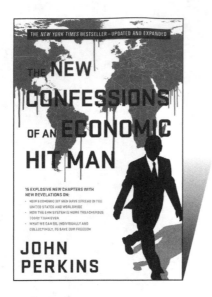

Featuring fifteen explosive new chapters, this expanded edition of a classic *New York Times* million-copy bestseller brings the story of economic hit men up to date and, chillingly, home to the United States. It also gives us hope and the tools to fight back.

In this astonishing tell-all book, former economic hit man (EHM) John Perkins shares new details about the ways he and others cheated countries around the globe out of trillions of dollars. Then he reveals how the deadly EHM cancer he helped create has spread far more widely and deeply than ever in the United States and everywhere else—to become the dominant system of business, government, and society today. Finally, he gives an insider view of what we each can do to change it.

Paperback, 384 pages, ISBN 978-1-62656-674-3
PDF ebook, ISBN 978-1-62656-675-0
ePub ebook, ISBN 978-1-62656-676-7

Berrett–Koehler Publishers, Inc.
www.bkconnection.com

800.929.2929

Dear reader,

Thank you for picking up this book and welcome to the worldwide BK community! You're joining a special group of people who have come together to create positive change in their lives, organizations, and communities.

What's BK all about?

Our mission is to connect people and ideas to create a world that works for all.

Why? Our communities, organizations, and lives get bogged down by old paradigms of self-interest, exclusion, hierarchy, and privilege. But we believe that can change. That's why we seek the leading experts on these challenges—and share their actionable ideas with you.

A welcome gift

To help you get started, we'd like to offer you a **free copy** of one of our bestselling ebooks:

www.bkconnection.com/welcome

When you claim your **free ebook**, you'll also be subscribed to our blog.

Our freshest insights

Access the best new tools and ideas for leaders at all levels on our blog at ideas.bkconnection.com.

Sincerely,

Your friends at Berrett-Koehler

Certified

Corporation